NO GALLBLADDER DIET COOKBOOK

2100 DAYS OF QUICK & EASY LOW-FAT MEALS TO BALANCE
YOUR METABOLISM AND ENHANCE YOUR DIGESTION | WITH
A 31-DAY MEAL PLAN FOR POST-SURGERY RECOVERY + 6
ESSENTIAL BONUSES

MARTHA MOSLEY

TABLE OF CONTENTS

INTRODUCTION

A New Beginning: What Losing Your Gallbladder Means for Your Digestion

When your gallbladder is removed, a significant shift occurs within your digestive system that necessitates adaptation. The gallbladder, though small, plays a pivotal role in digestion by storing bile produced by the liver. This bile helps in the digestion of fats, breaking them down into smaller droplets that enzymes in the intestines can more easily process. Without the gallbladder, bile flows directly from the liver into the small intestine, which can lead to digestive changes since bile isn't released in response to food but continuously.

Immediately after the gallbladder is removed, many people may experience changes in their digestion. One of the most common symptoms is diarrhea, which occurs because the bile, which is now constantly entering the intestine, can act as a laxative. Others might experience bloating, gas, or indigestion, especially after consuming fatty foods, because there is no longer a reservoir of bile to release in response to such foods. This can make it challenging to digest large amounts of fat at once, leading to discomfort.

Adapting to these changes often requires dietary adjustments. Reducing fat intake and eating smaller, more frequent meals can help manage symptoms by reducing the workload on the digestive system at any given time. Additionally, incorporating foods that are easy to digest and reducing those that cause gas or bloating—such as very spicy foods or some raw vegetables—can also ease the transition period post-surgery.

As you adapt to life without a gallbladder, understanding these changes is crucial. This cookbook aims to transform your approach to eating by offering recipes that cater to this new digestive reality. Each recipe is crafted to ensure that it is not only nutritious but also suitable for a system adjusting to the absence of a gallbladder. They focus on ingredients that are less likely to cause discomfort while still providing variety and satisfaction in your meals.

The importance of balancing your metabolism also becomes more pronounced after gallbladder removal. Your body has to process nutrients differently, particularly fats, which are crucial for energy. Balancing your diet with appropriate amounts of carbohydrates, proteins, and healthy fats is essential. Foods rich in soluble fiber, such as oatmeal, apples, and carrots, can help regulate the use of bile and assist in smoother digestion.

As you embark on this journey with this cookbook, you'll find a range of breakfast, lunch, and dinner recipes that align with these needs. For example, breakfast options might include avocado toast on whole grain bread, providing a good mix of healthy fats and fiber without overloading your digestive system. Lunches like a grilled chicken salad with mixed greens offer a high-protein, low-fat meal that is filling yet easy on the stomach. Dinners such as grilled salmon with steamed asparagus provide essential nutrients without the heavy fat content that could lead to discomfort.

Snacks and desserts are also designed with your new dietary needs in mind. They are easy to prepare and include ingredients that contribute positively to your digestive health. For instance, carrot and celery sticks with hummus provide a crunch and nutrients without the heaviness of traditional snack foods.

Beyond the recipes, this book includes a bonus chapter that serves as a crucial guide for your post-surgery journey. This section offers a 31-day meal plan carefully designed to ease your body into adjusting to its new normal. This meal plan includes a variety of recipes from the cookbook, ensuring that you have a balanced diet throughout the month. Additionally, there's a guide on foods to embrace and those to avoid, which simplifies grocery shopping and meal planning. This list helps mitigate the trial-and-error process that many face after surgery, providing a clear path to better health.

This cookbook not only aims to ease the physical transition after gallbladder removal but also addresses the emotional and psychological aspects. Adjusting to such a significant change can be daunting, and many people feel frustrated when conventional diets fail to consider their unique needs post-surgery. By offering recipes that are specifically designed for individuals without a gallbladder, this book provides not just nutritional guidance but also a sense of control and reassurance. It acknowledges that everyone's body reacts differently and emphasizes the importance of listening to your body and adjusting as needed.

Losing your gallbladder necessitates a careful reevaluation of your diet and lifestyle. This cookbook serves as a companion in your journey towards a balanced metabolism and enhanced digestion, providing you with the tools you need to adjust effectively and live comfortably without your gallbladder. With a variety of recipes and a comprehensive guide on managing your diet, it ensures that you can face the future with confidence and good health.

How This Cookbook Can Transform Your Diet and Health

When you undergo gallbladder removal, navigating your dietary needs becomes a pressing concern. This cookbook is designed to help you adapt smoothly and effectively, ensuring that you can maintain your health and enjoy delicious meals despite the changes your body is going through. The carefully crafted recipes and guidelines within this book cater specifically to those without a gallbladder, helping to mitigate common digestive issues while promoting overall health.

After gallbladder surgery, your body can no longer store bile, which plays a crucial role in the digestion of fats. This change can lead to digestive discomfort, especially after meals that are high in fat. Recognizing this, the recipes in this cookbook focus on low-fat ingredients that are less likely to cause distress. They are crafted to ensure that you can still enjoy a rich and varied diet, using ingredients that are both nourishing and gentle on your system.

The transformation in your diet begins with understanding the types of foods that your body can now handle more efficiently. This book includes a wealth of recipes that use lean proteins, whole grains, and plenty of fruits and vegetables. These ingredients form the basis of a healthy diet and are essential for someone adjusting to life without a gallbladder. By incorporating these foods into your daily meals, you can help stabilize your digestion and avoid the discomfort often associated with eating the wrong kinds of fats.

Moreover, this cookbook introduces meals that are not only easy to digest but also designed to be prepared with minimal effort. Recognizing that post-surgery life can be challenging, the recipes are straightforward and quick to prepare. This approach ensures that you can sustain a healthy diet even when you might not feel up to engaging in lengthy cooking processes. From smoothie bowls with papaya and chia seeds for breakfast to light-grilled salmon with steamed asparagus for dinner, the meals are balanced and can be made with ease.

An important aspect of this cookbook is its ability to educate. It doesn't just offer recipes; it also provides detailed explanations about why certain foods are recommended and how they benefit your health. For instance, it explains the role of soluble and insoluble fibers in aiding digestion and why complex carbohydrates are preferable to simple sugars. This educational approach empowers you with the knowledge to make informed choices about your diet beyond just following recipes.

The cookbook also addresses common post-surgery symptoms by including specific foods known to alleviate such conditions. For example, it suggests incorporating ginger and peppermint, which can help reduce nausea and soothe the stomach. These thoughtful inclusions ensure that the recipes are more than just food; they are also a form of natural remedy tailored to ease your transition and enhance your recovery.

In addition to the recipes and educational content, this cookbook offers a structured 31-day meal plan. This plan is invaluable for those just beginning to navigate their new dietary needs as it provides a clear, day-by-day guide to meals that support health and digestion. The meal plan helps eliminate the guesswork and anxiety about what to eat, providing you with a roadmap that ensures you get the nutrients your body needs to function optimally without the gallbladder.

The book also serves as a comprehensive guide, encompassing strategies for long-term dietary management without a gallbladder. It goes beyond immediate post-surgery care to address the ongoing adjustments you might need to make. This includes how to integrate your dietary needs with other lifestyle considerations, such as maintaining an active lifestyle or managing other health conditions.

By the time you reach the end of the cookbook, you'll find that it offers more than just recipes—it provides a new perspective on food and health. The combination of delicious, easy-to-prepare dishes and thorough nutritional guidance aims to transform your post-surgery diet into one that enhances your quality of life. It's about making each meal a step towards better health, ensuring that despite the absence of your gallbladder, you can lead a full, active, and satisfying life. This cookbook thus becomes not just a tool for adaptation but a companion in your journey toward a healthier, more comfortable future.

How Digestion Changes After Gallbladder Removal

After gallbladder removal, adapting to the long-term changes in digestion requires both understanding and careful management of one's diet. The gallbladder, although small, plays a crucial role in the digestive process, primarily in the storage and release of bile that helps in the breakdown of fats. Without this organ, bile from the liver drips continuously into the small intestine rather than being released in response to fatty foods. This alteration can lead to a series of digestive challenges and adjustments that are essential for maintaining health and comfort.

The immediate and most noticeable change often experienced post-surgery is an increase in the frequency and urgency of bowel movements, particularly after meals. This occurs because bile, which is now less concentrated and constantly entering the intestine, can irritate the lining of the digestive tract. For many, this results in diarrhea or softer stools. Additionally, without the gallbladder's capacity to regulate the flow of bile, digesting large amounts of fat at once becomes difficult. This often means that consuming the same foods as before the surgery, especially if they are high in fat, can lead to discomfort, bloating, and indigestion.

Dietary adjustments are necessary to manage these changes effectively. One of the first steps recommended is reducing the intake of fatty foods. This doesn't mean all fats need to be eliminated—fats are an essential part of a healthy diet—but it is important to limit the amount consumed at any one time and to choose sources of fat that are easier to digest. For instance, incorporating moderate amounts of healthy fats found in avocados, nuts, and olive oil can be beneficial compared to the fats found in fried foods or fatty cuts of meat.

Increasing fiber intake is another key adjustment. Fiber helps regulate the digestive system and can alleviate some of the symptoms of bile acid diarrhea, a common condition following gallbladder removal. Soluble fiber, in particular, found in foods like oatmeal, apples, and carrots, can bind with bile acid and help normalize bowel movements. However, it's crucial to increase fiber intake gradually, as adding too much too quickly can cause gas, bloating, and other digestive discomforts.

Moreover, eating smaller, more frequent meals can also help manage post-gallbladder removal symptoms. Smaller meals place less strain on the digestive system and can prevent the overwhelming release of bile that large meals might provoke. This approach not only helps in managing fat digestion but also stabilizes energy levels throughout the day.

Beyond adjusting the types of food eaten, the way in which foods are prepared is equally important. Steaming, grilling, and baking are preferable cooking methods over frying. These methods do not require large amounts of added fat and, thus, are more suitable for someone adjusting to life without a gallbladder. Additionally, it is advisable to be mindful of spicy foods and dairy products, as these can also exacerbate digestive symptoms in some individuals.

Long-term dietary management also involves careful monitoring and adaptation based on personal tolerance and response. This personalized approach is vital because everyone's body reacts differently post-surgery. Some may find they can tolerate a wider range of foods, while others might need to adhere more strictly to low-fat, high-fiber diets. Keeping a food diary can be a helpful tool in determining which foods trigger symptoms and which are well-tolerated.

It's not just about eliminating troublesome foods but also about incorporating a variety of nutrient-rich foods that support overall digestive health and well-being. Probiotics, for example, found in yogurt and fermented foods, can support gut health, helping to maintain a balanced intestinal flora, which is pivotal for a healthy digestive system. Meanwhile, ensuring adequate intake of vitamins and minerals supports the body's overall health, aiding in the recovery and maintenance phases post-surgery.

As these dietary adjustments become a routine part of life, it's also important for individuals to receive ongoing support and guidance. Regular consultations with nutritionists or dietitians can provide personalized advice and adjustments based on changing needs and conditions. This professional guidance ensures that the diet continues to support optimal health without the gallbladder, allowing individuals to lead a full and active life.

Living without a gallbladder certainly necessitates significant adjustments in one's dietary habits. Understanding these changes and how to manage them through diet can transform a potentially uncomfortable existence into a manageable and healthy lifestyle. By making informed choices about what to eat, how much to consume, and the best ways to prepare food, those without a gallbladder can continue to enjoy a diverse and satisfying diet while caring effectively for their digestive system.

The Importance of Balancing Your Metabolism

After gallbladder surgery, understanding and managing your metabolic health becomes a cornerstone of recovery and long-term well-being. The metabolism, a complex system that governs how your body converts food into energy, plays a critical role in your overall health. Its efficiency can affect everything from your energy levels to how well you digest food, particularly in the absence of your gallbladder.

The gallbladder's role in digestion is to store and concentrate bile produced by the liver, releasing it when you consume fat to aid in digestion. Without this reservoir, the bile flows directly into the intestines, which can lead to less efficient fat digestion and a host of digestive issues. This change means that your body must adapt not just to a missing organ but also to a new way of processing and metabolizing food, which can significantly impact your metabolic health.

One of the first challenges faced post-surgery is the management of bile acids. Without controlled release by the gallbladder, these acids can sometimes move too quickly through the intestines, which affects not only the digestion of fats but also the absorption of fat-soluble vitamins such as A, D, E, and K. These vitamins are crucial for a range of bodily functions, including bone health, blood clotting, and immune system performance. Their malabsorption can lead to deficiencies, affecting overall health and slowing recovery post-surgery. Therefore, balancing your diet to ensure adequate intake and absorption of these nutrients is essential.

Additionally, the continuous drip of bile can irritate the lining of the intestine, potentially leading to conditions such as bile acid diarrhea, which not only disrupts daily life but can also interfere with the absorption of essential nutrients. Managing these symptoms often requires a diet tailored to slow the transit time of food through the intestines and to bind bile acids. Foods rich in soluble fiber, such as oats, apples, and legumes, can help in this regard, illustrating the direct link between dietary choices, metabolic health, and digestive well-being.

Another aspect of metabolic health that becomes crucial after gallbladder removal is the regulation of blood sugar levels. The body's ability to manage and maintain stable blood sugar levels can be influenced by changes in food intake and digestion. For instance, a diet high in simple carbohydrates, which are quickly digested, can cause spikes in blood sugar. This can lead to increased fatigue and mood swings and, over time, can strain the pancreas and the liver, organs that are already compensating for the loss of the gallbladder. Therefore, incorporating complex carbohydrates and ensuring a balanced intake of proteins and fats are vital to stabilizing blood sugar and supporting overall metabolic health.

Maintaining a healthy weight is also an important aspect of managing metabolic health after gallbladder surgery. Weight fluctuations can occur if the diet is not adjusted to the body's new method of processing fats and other nutrients. Excessive weight gain, for instance, can put additional strain on the liver and pancreas, exacerbate issues like insulin resistance, and even lead to diabetes. Conversely, some individuals might experience weight loss if they excessively reduce their calorie intake due to fears of digestive discomfort. Ensuring a balanced, calorie-appropriate diet is thus essential for sustaining an optimal weight and metabolic rate.

Physical activity, coupled with dietary management, can also profoundly impact metabolic health. Regular exercise helps improve insulin sensitivity, manage body weight, and stimulate healthy digestion by literally moving the muscles around the gut. This can help alleviate some symptoms associated with poor digestion post-gallbladder removal, such as bloating and constipation, and promote a healthier metabolic rate.

Moreover, managing stress and ensuring adequate sleep are crucial components of maintaining metabolic health. Stress can disrupt digestive processes and exacerbate issues like irritable bowel syndrome, which can be more pronounced after gallbladder removal. Likewise, poor sleep can affect the hormones that regulate appetite and digestion, leading to poor dietary choices and compromised digestive health.

In essence, managing your metabolic health after gallbladder surgery is a multifaceted endeavor that involves a careful balance of diet, exercise, stress management, and regular medical check-ups. Each element plays a vital role in ensuring not just digestive comfort but also the overall functioning of your body's metabolic processes. Adapting to life without a gallbladder is not just about changing what you eat; it's about developing a comprehensive approach to how you maintain your body's health, ensuring that every calorie consumed contributes positively to your recovery and long-term well-being. By actively managing your metabolic health, you can enhance your quality of life even in the absence of this small but significant organ.

Thank You for Reading!

We hope you found the insights in this chapter both informative and beneficial as you navigate your post-surgery journey. Your feedback is invaluable to us and to others considering this book. If you have a moment, we would truly appreciate it if you could share your thoughts by leaving a review on Amazon.

Why Your Review Matters:

Your review helps us to improve and provide you with the best possible resource. It also assists others in the community to find and select resources that meet their needs, enabling them to benefit from shared experiences and advice.

How You Can Share Your Review:

Through Amazon.com:

- Go to the Amazon page where you found my book.
- Navigate to the 'Customer Reviews' section.
- Click on 'Write a customer review' to share your valuable insights.

Instant QR Code Access: Simply scan the QR code below with your smartphone to be directed to the Amazon review section.

BREAKFASTS

Avocado Toast on Whole Grain Bread

Ingredients:

- 1 ripe avocado
- 2 slices whole grain bread
- Salt and pepper to taste
- Optional: red pepper flakes, lemon juice

Directions:

1. Toast the whole grain bread to your preferred level of crispiness.
2. While the bread is toasting, mash the avocado in a bowl.
3. Add salt, pepper, and optional red pepper flakes or lemon juice to the mashed avocado.
4. Spread the avocado mixture evenly on the toasted bread slices.
5. Serve immediately and enjoy.

Nutritional Values (per serving):

- Calories: 250
- Fat: 15g
- Carbohydrates: 25g
- Protein: 5g

Spinach and Mushroom Egg White Omelette

Ingredients:

- 4 egg whites
- 1 cup fresh spinach
- 1/2 cup mushrooms, sliced
- 1 tablespoon olive oil
- Salt and pepper to taste

Directions:

1. Heat the olive oil in a non-stick skillet over medium heat.
2. Add the sliced mushrooms and cook until they begin to soften, about 3-4 minutes.
3. Add the spinach and cook until wilted.
4. Pour in the egg whites and let cook until they start to set, then gently fold the omelette.
5. Season with salt and pepper, then cook until the eggs are fully set.
6. Serve hot.

Nutritional Values (per serving):

- Calories: 120
- Fat: 7g
- Carbohydrates: 5g
- Protein: 12g

Banana Oatmeal Pancakes

Ingredients:

- 1 cup rolled oats
- 1 ripe banana
- 1 cup milk (dairy or non-dairy)
- 1 egg
- 1 teaspoon baking powder
- 1 teaspoon vanilla extract
- Optional: cinnamon, honey, or maple syrup for serving

Directions:

1. Blend the rolled oats in a blender until they become a fine flour.
2. In a mixing bowl, mash the banana and add the oat flour, milk, egg, baking powder, and vanilla extract.
3. Mix until well combined.
4. Heat a non-stick skillet over medium heat and pour in small amounts of batter to form pancakes.
5. Cook until bubbles form on the surface, then flip and cook the other side until golden brown.
6. Serve with optional toppings.

Nutritional Values (per serving):

- Calories: 200
- Fat: 5g
- Carbohydrates: 30g
- Protein: 6g

Greek Yogurt Parfait with Berries and Granola

Ingredients:

- 1 cup Greek yogurt
- 1/2 cup mixed berries (blueberries, strawberries, raspberries)
- 1/4 cup granola
- Optional: honey or maple syrup for drizzling

Directions:

1. In a glass or bowl, layer half of the Greek yogurt.
2. Add a layer of mixed berries and granola.
3. Repeat the layers with the remaining yogurt, berries, and granola.
4. Drizzle with honey or maple syrup if desired.
5. Serve immediately.

Nutritional Values (per serving):

- Calories: 250
- Fat: 8g
- Carbohydrates: 30g
- Protein: 14g

Smoothie Bowl with Papaya and Chia Seeds

Ingredients:

- 1 cup papaya, chopped
- 1 banana

- 1/2 cup almond milk
- 1 tablespoon chia seeds
- Optional toppings: fresh berries, granola, coconut flakes

Directions:

1. Blend the papaya, banana, and almond milk until smooth.
2. Pour the smoothie into a bowl.
3. Top with chia seeds and any optional toppings.
4. Serve immediately.

Nutritional Values (per serving):

- Calories: 220
- Fat: 6g
- Carbohydrates: 38g
- Protein: 4g

Baked Sweet Potato and Poached Eggs

Ingredients:

- 1 medium sweet potato
- 2 eggs
- 1 tablespoon olive oil
- Salt and pepper to taste

Directions:

1. Preheat the oven to 400°F (200°C).
2. Wash and slice the sweet potato into rounds.
3. Toss the sweet potato slices in olive oil, salt, and pepper.
4. Bake for 20-25 minutes or until tender.
5. While the sweet potato is baking, poach the eggs.
6. Serve the poached eggs on top of the baked sweet potato slices.

Nutritional Values (per serving):

- Calories: 300
- Fat: 15g
- Carbohydrates: 30g
- Protein: 12g

Turkey Sausage and Bell Pepper Scramble

Ingredients:

- 2 turkey sausages
- 1/2 cup bell peppers, diced
- 4 eggs
- 1 tablespoon olive oil
- Salt and pepper to taste

Directions:

1. Heat the olive oil in a skillet over medium heat.
2. Cook the turkey sausages until browned, then remove from the skillet and slice.
3. In the same skillet, sauté the bell peppers until tender.
4. Add the sliced sausage back to the skillet.

5. Beat the eggs in a bowl, then pour over the sausage and peppers.
6. Cook, stirring occasionally, until the eggs are fully cooked.
7. Season with salt and pepper and serve hot.

Nutritional Values (per serving):

- Calories: 350
- Fat: 25g
- Carbohydrates: 5g
- Protein: 25g

Quinoa Porridge with Almonds and Apple

Ingredients:

- 1/2 cup quinoa
- 1 cup almond milk
- 1 apple, chopped
- 1/4 cup sliced almonds
- 1 tablespoon honey
- 1/2 teaspoon cinnamon

Directions:

1. Rinse the quinoa thoroughly.
2. In a saucepan, combine quinoa and almond milk. Bring to a boil, then reduce to a simmer and cook until the quinoa is tender.
3. Stir in the chopped apple, almonds, honey, and cinnamon.
4. Serve warm.

Nutritional Values (per serving):

- Calories: 280
- Fat: 10g
- Carbohydrates: 40g
- Protein: 8g

Cottage Cheese with Pineapple and Mint

Ingredients:

- 1 cup cottage cheese
- 1/2 cup pineapple chunks
- 1 tablespoon fresh mint, chopped

Directions:

1. In a bowl, combine cottage cheese and pineapple chunks.
2. Sprinkle with chopped mint.
3. Serve chilled.

Nutritional Values (per serving):

- Calories: 180
- Fat: 5g
- Carbohydrates: 15g
- Protein: 20g

Vegan Blueberry Muffins

Ingredients:

- 1 cup flour
- 1/2 cup almond milk
- 1/2 cup sugar
- 1/4 cup coconut oil, melted
- 1 cup blueberries
- 1 teaspoon baking powder

- 1 teaspoon vanilla extract
- 1/4 teaspoon salt

Directions:

1. Preheat the oven to 375°F (190°C).
2. In a mixing bowl, combine flour, baking powder, and salt.
3. In another bowl, mix almond milk, sugar, melted coconut oil, and vanilla extract.
4. Combine the wet and dry ingredients, then fold in the blueberries.
5. Pour the batter into muffin tins and bake for 20-25 minutes or until a toothpick inserted into the center comes out clean.
6. Allow to cool before serving.

Nutritional Values (per serving):

- Calories: 150
- Fat: 7g
- Carbohydrates: 20g
- Protein: 2g

Tofu and Asparagus Frittata

Ingredients:

- 1 cup tofu, crumbled
- 1 cup asparagus, chopped
- 4 eggs
- 1/2 cup milk (dairy or non-dairy)
- 1 tablespoon olive oil

- Salt and pepper to taste

Directions:

1. Preheat the oven to 375°F (190°C).
2. Heat olive oil in an oven-safe skillet over medium heat.
3. Add chopped asparagus and cook until tender, about 5 minutes.
4. In a bowl, whisk together eggs, milk, salt, and pepper.
5. Add crumbled tofu to the skillet and mix with asparagus.
6. Pour the egg mixture over the tofu and asparagus, stirring gently to combine.
7. Transfer the skillet to the oven and bake for 15-20 minutes or until the eggs are set.
8. Serve warm.

Nutritional Values (per serving):

- Calories: 200
- Fat: 12g
- Carbohydrates: 6g
- Protein: 16g

Overnight Oats with Pumpkin Spice

Ingredients:

- 1/2 cup rolled oats
- 1/2 cup milk (dairy or non-dairy)
- 1/4 cup pumpkin puree

- 1 tablespoon chia seeds
- 1/2 teaspoon pumpkin spice
- 1 tablespoon maple syrup

Directions:

1. In a jar or bowl, combine rolled oats, milk, pumpkin puree, chia seeds, pumpkin spice, and maple syrup.
2. Stir well to combine.
3. Cover and refrigerate overnight.
4. In the morning, stir again and enjoy cold or warm.

Nutritional Values (per serving):

- Calories: 250
- Fat: 8g
- Carbohydrates: 40g
- Protein: 7g

Whole Wheat Pancakes with Strawberry Compote

Ingredients:

- 1 cup whole wheat flour
- 1 cup milk (dairy or non-dairy)
- 1 egg
- 1 tablespoon baking powder
- 1 teaspoon vanilla extract
- 1 cup strawberries, chopped
- 1 tablespoon sugar

Directions:

1. In a mixing bowl, combine whole wheat flour, milk, egg, baking powder, and vanilla extract.
2. Mix until well combined.
3. Heat a non-stick skillet over medium heat and pour in small amounts of batter to form pancakes.
4. Cook until bubbles form on the surface, then flip and cook the other side until golden brown.
5. In a small saucepan, combine strawberries and sugar. Cook over medium heat until strawberries break down into a compote.
6. Serve pancakes topped with strawberry compote.

Nutritional Values (per serving):

- Calories: 220
- Fat: 5g
- Carbohydrates: 40g
- Protein: 7g

Turkey Bacon and Avocado Wrap

Ingredients:

- 2 slices turkey bacon
- 1/2 avocado, sliced
- 1 whole grain wrap
- 1/2 cup mixed greens
- Salt and pepper to taste

Directions:

1. Cook turkey bacon in a skillet over medium heat until crispy.
2. Lay the whole grain wrap flat and place the mixed greens in the center.
3. Add the sliced avocado and turkey bacon on top of the greens.
4. Season with salt and pepper.
5. Roll up the wrap and slice in half.
6. Serve immediately.

Nutritional Values (per serving):

- Calories: 250
- Fat: 15g
- Carbohydrates: 25g
- Protein: 12g

Almond Butter and Banana Sandwich

Ingredients:

- 2 slices whole grain bread
- 2 tablespoons almond butter
- 1 banana, sliced

Directions:

1. Spread almond butter evenly on one slice of whole grain bread.
2. Arrange the banana slices on top of the almond butter.
3. Place the other slice of bread on top to form a sandwich.
4. Slice in half and serve.

Nutritional Values (per serving):

- Calories: 300
- Fat: 14g
- Carbohydrates: 38g
- Protein: 8g

Low-Fat Cheese and Tomato Quesadilla

Ingredients:

- 1 whole wheat tortilla
- 1/2 cup low-fat shredded cheese
- 1 tomato, sliced
- 1 tablespoon olive oil

Directions:

1. Heat olive oil in a skillet over medium heat.
2. Place the tortilla in the skillet and sprinkle one half with low-fat shredded cheese.
3. Arrange tomato slices on top of the cheese.
4. Fold the tortilla over and cook until the cheese is melted and the tortilla is crispy, flipping once.
5. Slice into wedges and serve.

Nutritional Values (per serving):

- Calories: 250
- Fat: 12g
- Carbohydrates: 24g
- Protein: 10g

Pear and Walnut Baked Oatmeal

Ingredients:

- 1 cup rolled oats
- 1 cup milk (dairy or non-dairy)
- 1 pear, chopped
- 1/4 cup walnuts, chopped
- 1 tablespoon maple syrup
- 1/2 teaspoon cinnamon

Directions:

1. Preheat the oven to 350°F (175°C).
2. In a mixing bowl, combine rolled oats, milk, chopped pear, walnuts, maple syrup, and cinnamon.
3. Pour the mixture into a baking dish.
4. Bake for 25-30 minutes or until the top is golden brown.
5. Serve warm.

Nutritional Values (per serving):

- Calories: 300
- Fat: 12g
- Carbohydrates: 42g
- Protein: 6g

Spinach and Feta Breakfast Burrito

Ingredients:

- 1 whole grain tortilla
- 2 eggs
- 1/2 cup fresh spinach
- 1/4 cup feta cheese, crumbled
- 1 tablespoon olive oil
- Salt and pepper to taste

Directions:

1. Heat olive oil in a skillet over medium heat.
2. Add spinach and cook until wilted.
3. Beat the eggs in a bowl, then pour into the skillet with the spinach. Cook, stirring, until the eggs are fully set.
4. Season with salt and pepper and remove from heat.
5. Place the scrambled eggs and spinach mixture in the center of the tortilla.
6. Sprinkle with crumbled feta cheese.
7. Roll up the tortilla to form a burrito.
8. Serve immediately.

Nutritional Values (per serving):

- Calories: 350
- Fat: 20g
- Carbohydrates: 28g
- Protein: 16g

Muesli with Skim Milk and Sliced Peach

Ingredients:

- 1 cup muesli

- 1 cup skim milk
- 1 peach, sliced

Directions:

1. In a bowl, combine muesli and skim milk.
2. Top with sliced peach.
3. Serve immediately.

Nutritional Values (per serving):

- Calories: 250
- Fat: 5g
- Carbohydrates: 42g
- Protein: 10g

Egg White and Spinach Breakfast Sandwich

Ingredients:

- 2 egg whites
- 1 whole grain English muffin
- 1/2 cup fresh spinach
- 1 slice low-fat cheese
- Salt and pepper to taste

Directions:

1. Toast the whole grain English muffin.
2. In a skillet over medium heat, cook the egg whites until fully set.
3. Add fresh spinach to the skillet and cook until wilted.
4. Place the cooked egg whites and spinach on one half of the toasted English muffin.
5. Top with a slice of low-fat cheese and the other half of the muffin.
6. Serve immediately.

Nutritional Values (per serving):

- Calories: 200
- Fat: 5g
- Carbohydrates: 28g
- Protein: 15g

LUNCHES

Grilled Chicken Salad with Mixed Greens

Ingredients:

- 1 chicken breast, grilled and sliced
- 4 cups mixed greens
- 1/2 cup cherry tomatoes, halved
- 1/4 cup red onion, thinly sliced
- 1/4 cup cucumber, sliced
- 2 tablespoons olive oil
- 1 tablespoon balsamic vinegar
- Salt and pepper to taste

Directions:

1. Grill the chicken breast until fully cooked and slice into strips.
2. In a large bowl, combine mixed greens, cherry tomatoes, red onion, and cucumber.
3. Top with grilled chicken slices.
4. Drizzle with olive oil and balsamic vinegar.
5. Season with salt and pepper and toss gently.
6. Serve immediately.

Nutritional Values (per serving):

- Calories: 350
- Fat: 20g
- Carbohydrates: 10g
- Protein: 30g

Quinoa and Black Bean Stuffed Peppers

Ingredients:

- 4 bell peppers, tops cut off and seeds removed
- 1 cup cooked quinoa
- 1 cup black beans, drained and rinsed
- 1/2 cup corn kernels
- 1/4 cup chopped cilantro
- 1/2 cup salsa
- 1/2 teaspoon cumin
- Salt and pepper to taste

Directions:

1. Preheat the oven to 375°F (190°C).
2. In a mixing bowl, combine cooked quinoa, black beans, corn, cilantro, salsa, cumin, salt, and pepper.
3. Stuff the mixture into the bell peppers.

4. Place the stuffed peppers in a baking dish and cover with foil.
5. Bake for 30 minutes or until the peppers are tender.
6. Serve hot.

Nutritional Values (per serving):

- Calories: 200
- Fat: 4g
- Carbohydrates: 35g
- Protein: 8g

Turkey and Hummus Wrap

Ingredients:

- 1 whole grain wrap
- 3 slices turkey breast
- 2 tablespoons hummus
- 1/2 cup mixed greens
- 1/4 cup shredded carrots

Directions:

1. Lay the whole grain wrap flat and spread hummus evenly over the surface.
2. Layer turkey slices, mixed greens, and shredded carrots on top.
3. Roll up the wrap tightly and slice in half.
4. Serve immediately.

Nutritional Values (per serving):

- Calories: 250
- Fat: 8g
- Carbohydrates: 28g
- Protein: 15g

Vegetable Lentil Soup

Ingredients:

- 1 cup lentils, rinsed
- 1 onion, chopped
- 2 carrots, chopped
- 2 celery stalks, chopped
- 1 zucchini, chopped
- 4 cups vegetable broth
- 1 tablespoon olive oil
- 1 teaspoon cumin
- 1 teaspoon paprika
- Salt and pepper to taste

Directions:

1. Heat olive oil in a large pot over medium heat.
2. Add onion, carrots, and celery, and cook until softened, about 5 minutes.
3. Stir in zucchini, cumin, and paprika, and cook for another 2 minutes.
4. Add lentils and vegetable broth.
5. Bring to a boil, then reduce heat and simmer for 30 minutes or until lentils are tender.
6. Season with salt and pepper.
7. Serve hot.

Nutritional Values (per serving):

- Calories: 180
- Fat: 5g
- Carbohydrates: 30g
- Protein: 10g

Tuna Salad Stuffed Avocado

Ingredients:

- 2 ripe avocados, halved and pitted
- 1 can tuna, drained
- 1/4 cup Greek yogurt
- 1 tablespoon lemon juice
- 1 celery stalk, chopped
- Salt and pepper to taste

Directions:

1. In a bowl, mix tuna, Greek yogurt, lemon juice, chopped celery, salt, and pepper.
2. Scoop a portion of the tuna salad into each avocado half.
3. Serve immediately.

Nutritional Values (per serving):

- Calories: 300
- Fat: 20g
- Carbohydrates: 10g
- Protein: 20g

Veggie and Goat Cheese Flatbread

Ingredients:

- 1 whole grain flatbread
- 1/2 cup goat cheese, crumbled
- 1/2 cup cherry tomatoes, halved
- 1/4 cup red onion, thinly sliced
- 1/4 cup spinach leaves
- 1 tablespoon olive oil
- Salt and pepper to taste

Directions:

1. Preheat the oven to 400°F (200°C).
2. Place the flatbread on a baking sheet.
3. Spread goat cheese evenly over the flatbread.
4. Top with cherry tomatoes, red onion, and spinach leaves.
5. Drizzle with olive oil and season with salt and pepper.
6. Bake for 10-12 minutes or until the flatbread is crispy and the toppings are tender.
7. Serve hot.

Nutritional Values (per serving):

- Calories: 300
- Fat: 15g
- Carbohydrates: 30g
- Protein: 10g

Spiced Lentil and Carrot Salad

Ingredients:

- 1 cup cooked lentils
- 2 carrots, grated
- 1/4 cup raisins
- 2 tablespoons olive oil
- 1 tablespoon lemon juice
- 1 teaspoon cumin
- 1/2 teaspoon cinnamon
- Salt and pepper to taste

Directions:

1. In a large bowl, combine cooked lentils, grated carrots, and raisins.
2. In a small bowl, whisk together olive oil, lemon juice, cumin, cinnamon, salt, and pepper.
3. Pour the dressing over the lentil mixture and toss to combine.
4. Serve chilled or at room temperature.

Nutritional Values (per serving):

- Calories: 220
- Fat: 8g
- Carbohydrates: 32g
- Protein: 6g

Grilled Shrimp and Mango Salad

Ingredients:

- 1 cup shrimp, peeled and deveined
- 1 mango, diced
- 4 cups mixed greens
- 1/4 cup red onion, thinly sliced
- 2 tablespoons olive oil
- 1 tablespoon lime juice
- Salt and pepper to taste

Directions:

- Heat a grill pan over medium heat and lightly coat with olive oil.
- Grill shrimp until pink and cooked through, about 2-3 minutes per side.
- In a large bowl, combine mixed greens, diced mango, and red onion.
- Add grilled shrimp to the salad.
- In a small bowl, whisk together olive oil, lime juice, salt, and pepper.
- Drizzle the dressing over the salad and toss gently.
- Serve immediately.

Nutritional Values (per serving):

- Calories: 250
- Fat: 14g
- Carbohydrates: 20g
- Protein: 12g

Baked Falafel with Tzatziki Sauce

Ingredients:

- 1 cup chickpeas, drained and rinsed
- 1/4 cup onion, chopped
- 2 garlic cloves
- 1/4 cup fresh parsley
- 1 teaspoon cumin
- 1 teaspoon coriander
- 1 tablespoon olive oil
- Salt and pepper to taste

Tzatziki Sauce:

- 1/2 cup Greek yogurt
- 1/4 cucumber, grated
- 1 tablespoon lemon juice
- 1 garlic clove, minced
- Salt and pepper to taste

Directions:

1. Preheat the oven to 375°F (190°C).
2. In a food processor, combine chickpeas, onion, garlic, parsley, cumin, coriander, olive oil, salt, and pepper. Blend until smooth.
3. Form the mixture into small patties and place on a baking sheet lined with parchment paper.
4. Bake for 20-25 minutes or until golden brown and crispy.
5. Meanwhile, prepare the tzatziki sauce by mixing Greek yogurt, grated cucumber, lemon juice, minced garlic, salt, and pepper in a bowl.
6. Serve the baked falafel with the tzatziki sauce.

Nutritional Values (per serving):

- Calories: 200
- Fat: 8g
- Carbohydrates: 26g
- Protein: 8g

Roast Beef and Horseradish Wrap

Ingredients:

- 1 whole grain wrap
- 4 slices roast beef
- 1 tablespoon horseradish sauce
- 1/2 cup mixed greens
- 1/4 cup shredded carrots

Directions:

1. Lay the whole grain wrap flat and spread horseradish sauce evenly over the surface.
2. Layer roast beef slices, mixed greens, and shredded carrots on top.
3. Roll up the wrap tightly and slice in half.
4. Serve immediately.

Nutritional Values (per serving):

- Calories: 300
- Fat: 10g
- Carbohydrates: 25g
- Protein: 20g

Vegetable Stir-Fry with Brown Rice

Ingredients:

- 1 cup cooked brown rice
- 1 bell pepper, sliced
- 1 carrot, sliced
- 1 zucchini, sliced
- 1 cup broccoli florets

- 2 tablespoons soy sauce
- 1 tablespoon olive oil
- 1 garlic clove, minced
- 1 teaspoon ginger, minced

Directions:

1. Heat olive oil in a large skillet or wok over medium-high heat.
2. Add garlic and ginger, and sauté for 1 minute.
3. Add bell pepper, carrot, zucchini, and broccoli. Stir-fry until vegetables are tender, about 5-7 minutes.
4. Add soy sauce and cooked brown rice, and stir until everything is well combined and heated through.
5. Serve hot.

Nutritional Values (per serving):

- Calories: 250
- Fat: 7g
- Carbohydrates: 40g
- Protein: 6g

Pasta Primavera with Olive Oil

Ingredients:

- 8 ounces whole wheat pasta
- 1 cup cherry tomatoes, halved
- 1 zucchini, sliced
- 1 yellow squash, sliced
- 1/2 cup peas
- 2 tablespoons olive oil

- 2 garlic cloves, minced
- 1/4 cup grated Parmesan cheese
- Salt and pepper to taste

Directions:

1. Cook the whole wheat pasta according to package instructions. Drain and set aside.
2. Heat olive oil in a large skillet over medium heat.
3. Add garlic and sauté until fragrant, about 1 minute.
4. Add cherry tomatoes, zucchini, yellow squash, and peas. Cook until vegetables are tender, about 5 minutes.
5. Toss the cooked pasta with the vegetables and olive oil.
6. Season with salt and pepper, and sprinkle with grated Parmesan cheese.
7. Serve hot.

Nutritional Values (per serving):

- Calories: 350
- Fat: 12g
- Carbohydrates: 52g
- Protein: 12g

Spinach and Quinoa Power Bowl

Ingredients:

- 1 cup cooked quinoa
- 2 cups fresh spinach

- 1/2 cup cherry tomatoes, halved
- 1/4 cup red onion, sliced
- 1/4 cup feta cheese, crumbled
- 2 tablespoons olive oil
- 1 tablespoon lemon juice
- Salt and pepper to taste

Directions:

1. In a large bowl, combine cooked quinoa, fresh spinach, cherry tomatoes, red onion, and feta cheese.
2. In a small bowl, whisk together olive oil, lemon juice, salt, and pepper.
3. Drizzle the dressing over the quinoa and vegetables, and toss to combine.
4. Serve immediately.

Nutritional Values (per serving):

- Calories: 300
- Fat: 16g
- Carbohydrates: 32g
- Protein: 10g

Tomato Basil Soup with a Mozzarella Toast

Ingredients:

- 1 tablespoon olive oil
- 1 onion, chopped
- 2 garlic cloves, minced
- 4 cups chopped tomatoes
- 2 cups vegetable broth
- 1/4 cup fresh basil, chopped
- Salt and pepper to taste
- 4 slices whole grain bread
- 1/2 cup shredded mozzarella cheese

Directions:

1. Heat olive oil in a large pot over medium heat.
2. Add onion and garlic, and sauté until softened, about 5 minutes.
3. Add chopped tomatoes and vegetable broth. Bring to a boil, then reduce heat and simmer for 20 minutes.
4. Use an immersion blender to puree the soup until smooth.
5. Stir in fresh basil, and season with salt and pepper.
6. Meanwhile, toast the whole grain bread slices and top with shredded mozzarella cheese. Place under a broiler until the cheese is melted.
7. Serve the soup hot with a mozzarella toast on the side.

Nutritional Values (per serving):

- Calories: 350
- Fat: 14g
- Carbohydrates: 40g
- Protein: 15g

Turkey and Spinach Panini with Pesto

Ingredients:

- 2 slices whole grain bread

- 3 slices turkey breast
- 1/2 cup fresh spinach
- 1 tablespoon pesto
- 1 slice provolone cheese

Directions:

1. Preheat a panini press or skillet.
2. Spread pesto on one slice of bread.
3. Layer turkey, spinach, and provolone cheese on top.
4. Top with the second slice of bread.
5. Grill the sandwich in the panini press or skillet until the bread is toasted and the cheese is melted.
6. Serve hot.

Nutritional Values (per serving):

- Calories: 350
- Fat: 14g
- Carbohydrates: 30g
- Protein: 20g

Zucchini Noodles with Pesto and Cherry Tomatoes

Ingredients:

1. 2 medium zucchinis, spiralized into noodles
2. 1 cup cherry tomatoes, halved
3. 1/4 cup pesto
4. 1 tablespoon olive oil
5. Salt and pepper to taste

Directions:

- Heat olive oil in a large skillet over medium heat.
- Add zucchini noodles and cook for 2-3 minutes until tender.
- Add cherry tomatoes and cook for another 2 minutes.
- Remove from heat and toss with pesto.
- Season with salt and pepper.
- Serve immediately.

Nutritional Values (per serving):

- Calories: 200
- Fat: 14g
- Carbohydrates: 12g
- Protein: 4g

Sushi Rolls with Avocado and Cucumber

Ingredients:

- 1 cup sushi rice, cooked
- 2 tablespoons rice vinegar
- 4 nori sheets
- 1 avocado, sliced
- 1 cucumber, sliced into strips
- Soy sauce for dipping

Directions:

1. Mix cooked sushi rice with rice vinegar.
2. Place a nori sheet on a bamboo mat, shiny side down.

3. Spread a thin layer of rice over the nori, leaving a 1-inch border at the top.
4. Place avocado slices and cucumber strips across the middle of the rice.
5. Roll the bamboo mat tightly to form a roll, using the border to seal the roll.
6. Slice into bite-sized pieces.
7. Serve with soy sauce for dipping.

Nutritional Values (per serving):

- Calories: 250
- Fat: 8g
- Carbohydrates: 38g
- Protein: 4g

Chicken Caesar Salad with Low-Fat Dressing

Ingredients:

- 1 chicken breast, grilled and sliced
- 4 cups romaine lettuce, chopped
- 1/4 cup grated Parmesan cheese
- 1/2 cup croutons
- 1/4 cup low-fat Caesar dressing

Directions:

1. In a large bowl, combine romaine lettuce, grated Parmesan cheese, and croutons.

2. Add grilled chicken slices on top.
3. Drizzle with low-fat Caesar dressing.
4. Toss gently to combine.
5. Serve immediately.

Nutritional Values (per serving):

- Calories: 350
- Fat: 14g
- Carbohydrates: 20g
- Protein: 30g

Cold Rice Noodle Salad with Peanut Lime Dressing

Ingredients:

- 8 ounces rice noodles
- 1 cup shredded carrots
- 1 cup sliced bell peppers
- 1/2 cup chopped cilantro
- 1/4 cup chopped peanuts

Peanut Lime Dressing:

- 3 tablespoons peanut butter
- 2 tablespoons soy sauce
- 1 tablespoon lime juice
- 1 tablespoon honey
- 1 garlic clove, minced
- 1/2 teaspoon ginger, minced

Directions:

1. Cook rice noodles according to package instructions. Drain and rinse with cold water.

2. In a bowl, whisk together peanut butter, soy sauce, lime juice, honey, garlic, and ginger until smooth.
3. In a large bowl, combine rice noodles, shredded carrots, sliced bell peppers, and chopped cilantro.
4. Pour the dressing over the noodle mixture and toss to combine.
5. Sprinkle with chopped peanuts before serving.
6. Serve chilled.

Nutritional Values (per serving):

- Calories: 350
- Fat: 12g
- Carbohydrates: 50g
- Protein: 8g

Mediterranean Chickpea and Cucumber Wrap

Ingredients:

- 1 whole grain wrap
- 1/2 cup chickpeas, drained and rinsed
- 1/2 cup cucumber, diced
- 1/4 cup red onion, diced
- 1/4 cup feta cheese, crumbled
- 2 tablespoons hummus
- 1 tablespoon lemon juice
- Salt and pepper to taste

Directions:

1. In a bowl, combine chickpeas, cucumber, red onion, feta cheese, lemon juice, salt, and pepper.
2. Spread hummus on the whole grain wrap.
3. Add the chickpea mixture on top of the hummus.
4. Roll up the wrap tightly and slice in half.
5. Serve immediately.

Nutritional Values (per serving):

- Calories: 300
- Fat: 10g
- Carbohydrates: 40g
- Protein: 12g

Grilled Vegetable and Hummus Tartine

Ingredients:

- 1 slice whole grain bread
- 1/4 cup hummus
- 1/2 cup grilled vegetables (zucchini, bell peppers, eggplant)
- 1 tablespoon olive oil
- Salt and pepper to taste

Directions:

1. Grill the vegetables until tender, brushing with olive oil and seasoning with salt and pepper.

2. Toast the whole grain bread.
3. Spread hummus on the toasted bread.
4. Top with grilled vegetables.
5. Serve immediately.

Nutritional Values (per serving):

- Calories: 250
- Fat: 12g
- Carbohydrates: 28g
- Protein: 6g

Sweet Potato and Black Bean Burrito

Ingredients:

- 1 whole grain tortilla
- 1/2 cup black beans, drained and rinsed
- 1 small sweet potato, cooked and mashed
- 1/4 cup corn kernels
- 1/4 cup salsa
- 1/4 cup shredded cheddar cheese
- 1 tablespoon olive oil
- 1 teaspoon cumin
- Salt and pepper to taste

Directions:

1. Heat olive oil in a skillet over medium heat.
2. Add black beans, corn, cumin, salt, and pepper. Cook until heated through.
3. Warm the tortilla in a separate skillet.
4. Spread mashed sweet potato on the tortilla.
5. Add the black bean mixture on top of the sweet potato.
6. Sprinkle with shredded cheddar cheese and salsa.
7. Roll up the tortilla to form a burrito.
8. Serve immediately.

Nutritional Values (per serving):

- Calories: 350
- Fat: 14g
- Carbohydrates: 48g
- Protein: 12g

Smoked Salmon and Cream Cheese Bagel

Ingredients:

- 1 whole grain bagel
- 2 tablespoons low-fat cream cheese
- 2 ounces smoked salmon
- 1/4 cup red onion, thinly sliced
- 1 tablespoon capers
- Fresh dill for garnish

Directions:

1. Toast the whole grain bagel.
2. Spread low-fat cream cheese on each half of the bagel.
3. Layer smoked salmon on top of the cream cheese.

4. Add thinly sliced red onion and capers.
5. Garnish with fresh dill.
6. Serve immediately.

Nutritional Values (per serving):

- Calories: 300
- Fat: 10g
- Carbohydrates: 35g
- Protein: 18g

Asian Chicken Lettuce Wraps

Ingredients:

- 1 pound ground chicken
- 1/2 cup water chestnuts, chopped
- 1/2 cup mushrooms, chopped
- 1/4 cup green onions, chopped
- 1 tablespoon soy sauce
- 1 tablespoon hoisin sauce
- 1 tablespoon sesame oil
- 1 garlic clove, minced
- 1 head butter lettuce, leaves separated

Directions:

1. Heat sesame oil in a skillet over medium heat.
2. Add garlic and cook until fragrant, about 1 minute.
3. Add ground chicken and cook until browned, breaking it up with a spoon.

4. Stir in water chestnuts, mushrooms, green onions, soy sauce, and hoisin sauce. Cook until the vegetables are tender, about 5 minutes.
5. Spoon the chicken mixture into lettuce leaves.
6. Serve immediately.

Nutritional Values (per serving):

- Calories: 250
- Fat: 15g
- Carbohydrates: 10g
- Protein: 20g

Greek Salad with Chicken and Low-Fat Feta

Ingredients:

- 1 chicken breast, grilled and sliced
- 4 cups romaine lettuce, chopped
- 1/2 cup cherry tomatoes, halved
- 1/4 cup red onion, sliced
- 1/4 cup cucumber, sliced
- 1/4 cup low-fat feta cheese, crumbled
- 2 tablespoons olive oil
- 1 tablespoon red wine vinegar
- Salt and pepper to taste

Directions:

1. In a large bowl, combine romaine lettuce, cherry

tomatoes, red onion, cucumber, and low-fat feta cheese.
2. Top with grilled chicken slices.
3. In a small bowl, whisk together olive oil, red wine vinegar, salt, and pepper.
4. Drizzle the dressing over the salad and toss gently.
5. Serve immediately.

Nutritional Values (per serving):

- Calories: 350
- Fat: 18g
- Carbohydrates: 10g
- Protein: 30g

DINNERS

Grilled Salmon with Steamed Asparagus

Ingredients:

- 2 salmon fillets
- 1 bunch asparagus, trimmed
- 2 tablespoons olive oil
- 1 lemon, sliced
- Salt and pepper to taste

Directions:

1. Preheat the grill to medium-high heat.
2. Brush the salmon fillets with olive oil and season with salt and pepper.
3. Grill the salmon for about 4-5 minutes per side, or until cooked through.
4. Meanwhile, steam the asparagus until tender, about 3-4 minutes.
5. Serve the grilled salmon with steamed asparagus and lemon slices on the side.

Nutritional Values (per serving):

- Calories: 350
- Fat: 20g
- Carbohydrates: 5g

- Protein: 35g

Baked Cod with Lemon and Herbs

Ingredients:

- 2 cod fillets
- 1 lemon, sliced
- 2 tablespoons olive oil
- 1 tablespoon fresh parsley, chopped
- 1 teaspoon dried thyme
- Salt and pepper to taste

Directions:

1. Preheat the oven to 375°F (190°C).
2. Place cod fillets in a baking dish.
3. Drizzle with olive oil and season with salt, pepper, dried thyme, and fresh parsley.
4. Arrange lemon slices on top of the fish.
5. Bake for 15-20 minutes or until the fish flakes easily with a fork.
6. Serve hot.

Nutritional Values (per serving):

- Calories: 220

- Fat: 10g
- Carbohydrates: 2g
- Protein: 30g

Vegetable Paella

Ingredients:

- 1 cup arborio rice
- 1 bell pepper, chopped
- 1 zucchini, chopped
- 1 cup green beans, trimmed and chopped
- 1 onion, chopped
- 2 garlic cloves, minced
- 3 cups vegetable broth
- 1 tablespoon olive oil
- 1 teaspoon smoked paprika
- 1/2 teaspoon saffron threads
- Salt and pepper to taste

Directions:

1. Heat olive oil in a large skillet or paella pan over medium heat.
2. Add onion and garlic, and sauté until softened, about 5 minutes.
3. Stir in bell pepper, zucchini, and green beans, and cook for another 5 minutes.
4. Add arborio rice, smoked paprika, and saffron threads, and stir to combine.
5. Pour in vegetable broth and bring to a boil.
6. Reduce heat to low, cover, and simmer for 20-25 minutes, or until the rice is tender and the liquid is absorbed.
7. Season with salt and pepper, and serve hot.

Nutritional Values (per serving):

- Calories: 300
- Fat: 8g
- Carbohydrates: 52g
- Protein: 6g

Turkey Meatballs with Spaghetti Squash

Ingredients:

- 1 medium spaghetti squash
- 1 pound ground turkey
- 1/4 cup breadcrumbs
- 1/4 cup Parmesan cheese, grated
- 1 egg
- 2 garlic cloves, minced
- 1 teaspoon dried oregano
- Salt and pepper to taste
- 2 cups marinara sauce

Directions:

1. Preheat the oven to 375°F (190°C).
2. Cut the spaghetti squash in half lengthwise and remove the seeds. Place cut side down on a baking sheet and bake for 30-40 minutes, or until tender.
3. In a bowl, combine ground turkey, breadcrumbs, Parmesan

cheese, egg, garlic, oregano, salt, and pepper. Mix well and form into meatballs.

4. Place the meatballs on a baking sheet and bake for 20-25 minutes, or until cooked through.
5. In a saucepan, heat marinara sauce over medium heat.
6. Use a fork to scrape the spaghetti squash into strands.
7. Serve the turkey meatballs over the spaghetti squash strands with marinara sauce on top.

Nutritional Values (per serving):

- Calories: 350
- Fat: 12g
- Carbohydrates: 30g
- Protein: 30g

Grilled Tofu with a Ginger Soy Glaze

Ingredients:

- 1 block firm tofu, drained and pressed
- 1/4 cup soy sauce
- 2 tablespoons honey
- 1 tablespoon ginger, grated
- 1 garlic clove, minced
- 1 tablespoon sesame oil
- 1 green onion, chopped

Directions:

1. Cut the tofu into- 1/2-inch thick slices.
2. In a bowl, whisk together soy sauce, honey, grated ginger, minced garlic, and sesame oil.
3. Marinate the tofu slices in the soy sauce mixture for at least 30 minutes.
4. Preheat the grill to medium-high heat.
5. Grill the tofu slices for 3-4 minutes per side, or until grill marks appear.
6. Garnish with chopped green onion and serve immediately.

Nutritional Values (per serving):

- Calories: 200
- Fat: 10g
- Carbohydrates: 15g
- Protein: 15g

Chicken and Broccoli Alfredo with Whole Wheat Pasta

Ingredients:

- 8 ounces whole wheat pasta
- 1 cup broccoli florets
- 1 chicken breast, cooked and sliced
- 1 cup low-fat milk
- 1/2 cup Parmesan cheese, grated
- 2 tablespoons flour

- 2 tablespoons olive oil
- 2 garlic cloves, minced
- Salt and pepper to taste

Directions:

1. Cook whole wheat pasta according to package instructions. Drain and set aside.
2. Steam broccoli florets until tender, about 5 minutes.
3. In a saucepan, heat olive oil over medium heat. Add minced garlic and cook until fragrant, about 1 minute.
4. Whisk in flour and cook for another minute.
5. Gradually whisk in low-fat milk, stirring constantly until the sauce thickens.
6. Stir in Parmesan cheese, salt, and pepper.
7. Add cooked chicken slices and steamed broccoli to the sauce.
8. Toss the sauce with the cooked pasta.
9. Serve hot.

Nutritional Values (per serving):

- Calories: 400
- Fat: 14g
- Carbohydrates: 45g
- Protein: 25g

Beef Stir Fry with Bell Peppers and Broccoli

Ingredients:

- 1 pound beef sirloin, thinly sliced
- 1 bell pepper, sliced
- 1 cup broccoli florets
- 1/4 cup soy sauce
- 2 tablespoons hoisin sauce
- 1 tablespoon sesame oil
- 2 garlic cloves, minced
- 1 teaspoon ginger, minced
- 1 green onion, chopped

Directions:

1. Heat sesame oil in a large skillet or wok over medium-high heat.
2. Add garlic and ginger, and sauté for 1 minute.
3. Add beef slices and cook until browned, about 3-4 minutes.
4. Add bell pepper and broccoli florets, and cook until vegetables are tender, about 5 minutes.
5. Stir in soy sauce and hoisin sauce, and cook for another 2 minutes.
6. Garnish with chopped green onion and serve hot.

Nutritional Values (per serving):

- Calories: 350
- Fat: 18g

- Carbohydrates: 15g
- Protein: 30g

Moroccan Vegetable Tagine

Ingredients:

- 1 cup chickpeas, drained and rinsed
- 1 bell pepper, chopped
- 1 zucchini, chopped
- 1 carrot, chopped
- 1 onion, chopped
- 2 garlic cloves, minced
- 2 cups vegetable broth
- 1 tablespoon olive oil
- 1 teaspoon ground cumin
- 1 teaspoon ground cinnamon
- 1/2 teaspoon ground turmeric
- Salt and pepper to taste
- 1/4 cup fresh cilantro, chopped

Directions:

1. Heat olive oil in a large pot over medium heat.
2. Add onion and garlic, and sauté until softened, about 5 minutes.
3. Stir in bell pepper, zucchini, and carrot, and cook for another 5 minutes.
4. Add chickpeas, vegetable broth, ground cumin, ground cinnamon, ground turmeric, salt, and pepper.
5. Bring to a boil, then reduce heat and simmer for 20-25 minutes, or until vegetables are tender.
6. Garnish with fresh cilantro and serve hot.

Nutritional Values (per serving):

- Calories: 250
- Fat: 8g
- Carbohydrates: 38g
- Protein: 8g

Lemon Herb Roasted Chicken

Ingredients:

- 1 whole chicken
- 2 lemons, sliced
- 4 garlic cloves, minced
- 2 tablespoons olive oil
- 1 tablespoon fresh rosemary, chopped
- 1 tablespoon fresh thyme, chopped
- Salt and pepper to taste

Directions:

1. Preheat the oven to 375°F (190°C).
2. Place lemon slices inside the cavity of the chicken.
3. In a small bowl, mix minced garlic, olive oil, fresh rosemary, fresh thyme, salt, and pepper.
4. Rub the garlic and herb mixture all over the chicken.
5. Place the chicken in a roasting pan and roast for 1 hour and 30 minutes, or until the internal

temperature reaches 165°F (75°C).

6. Let the chicken rest for 10 minutes before carving.
7. Serve hot.

Nutritional Values (per serving):

- Calories: 400
- Fat: 25g
- Carbohydrates: 5g
- Protein: 35g

Vegan Chili

Ingredients:

- 1 cup black beans, drained and rinsed
- 1 cup kidney beans, drained and rinsed
- 1 bell pepper, chopped
- 1 onion, chopped
- 2 garlic cloves, minced
- 2 cups diced tomatoes
- 1 cup corn kernels
- 2 cups vegetable broth
- 2 tablespoons chili powder
- 1 teaspoon cumin
- 1 teaspoon paprika
- 1 tablespoon olive oil
- Salt and pepper to taste

Directions:

1. Heat olive oil in a large pot over medium heat.
2. Add onion and garlic, and sauté until softened, about 5 minutes.

3. Stir in bell pepper and cook for another 5 minutes.
4. Add black beans, kidney beans, diced tomatoes, corn, vegetable broth, chili powder, cumin, paprika, salt, and pepper.
5. Bring to a boil, then reduce heat and simmer for 30 minutes, or until the chili thickens.
6. Serve hot.

Nutritional Values (per serving):

- Calories: 300
- Fat: 8g
- Carbohydrates: 45g
- Protein: 12g

Roasted Eggplant and Spinach Lasagna

Ingredients:

- 2 large eggplants, sliced
- 1 cup ricotta cheese
- 1 cup mozzarella cheese, shredded
- 1/2 cup Parmesan cheese, grated
- 2 cups spinach, chopped
- 2 cups marinara sauce
- 1 egg
- 1 tablespoon olive oil
- Salt and pepper to taste

Directions:

1. Preheat the oven to 375°F (190°C).

2. Arrange eggplant slices on a baking sheet, drizzle with olive oil, and season with salt and pepper. Roast for 20 minutes or until tender.
3. In a bowl, combine ricotta cheese, chopped spinach, egg, salt, and pepper.
4. Spread a layer of marinara sauce on the bottom of a baking dish. Layer with roasted eggplant slices, ricotta mixture, and shredded mozzarella. Repeat layers, ending with marinara sauce and a sprinkle of Parmesan cheese on top.
5. Bake for 30 minutes or until bubbly and golden brown.
6. Let cool for 10 minutes before serving.

Nutritional Values (per serving):

- Calories: 300
- Fat: 15g
- Carbohydrates: 20g
- Protein: 15g

Pork Tenderloin with Apple Cider Reduction

Ingredients:

- 1 pound pork tenderloin
- 1 cup apple cider
- 2 tablespoons Dijon mustard
- 1 tablespoon olive oil
- 1 garlic clove, minced
- 1 teaspoon thyme
- Salt and pepper to taste

Directions:

1. Preheat the oven to 375°F (190°C).
2. Season pork tenderloin with salt, pepper, and thyme.
3. In a skillet, heat olive oil over medium-high heat. Sear the pork on all sides until browned.
4. Transfer the pork to a baking dish and roast for 20-25 minutes, or until the internal temperature reaches 145°F (63°C).
5. In the same skillet, add apple cider, Dijon mustard, and minced garlic. Cook until the sauce reduces by half.
6. Slice the pork tenderloin and drizzle with apple cider reduction.
7. Serve hot.

Nutritional Values (per serving):

- Calories: 250
- Fat: 10g
- Carbohydrates: 10g
- Protein: 30g

Butternut Squash Risotto

Ingredients:

- 1 cup arborio rice
- 2 cups butternut squash, diced
- 4 cups vegetable broth

- 1/2 cup Parmesan cheese, grated
- 1/4 cup white wine
- 1 onion, chopped
- 2 garlic cloves, minced
- 2 tablespoons olive oil
- 1 tablespoon butter
- Salt and pepper to taste

Directions:

1. Heat olive oil in a large pot over medium heat. Add onion and garlic, and sauté until softened, about 5 minutes.
2. Add diced butternut squash and cook for another 5 minutes.
3. Stir in arborio rice and cook for 2 minutes.
4. Pour in white wine and cook until absorbed.
5. Gradually add vegetable broth, one cup at a time, stirring constantly until the liquid is absorbed before adding more.
6. Once the rice is tender and creamy, stir in Parmesan cheese and butter. Season with salt and pepper.
7. Serve hot.

Nutritional Values (per serving):

- Calories: 350
- Fat: 14g
- Carbohydrates: 50g
- Protein: 10g

Cauliflower Steak with Olive Relish

Ingredients:

- 1 head cauliflower, sliced into steaks
- 1/4 cup olives, chopped
- 1 tablespoon capers
- 2 tablespoons parsley, chopped
- 2 tablespoons olive oil
- 1 lemon, juiced
- Salt and pepper to taste

Directions:

1. Preheat the oven to 400°F (200°C).
2. Brush cauliflower steaks with olive oil and season with salt and pepper. Roast for 20-25 minutes, or until tender and golden brown.
3. In a bowl, combine chopped olives, capers, parsley, olive oil, and lemon juice. Mix well.
4. Spoon the olive relish over the roasted cauliflower steaks.
5. Serve immediately.

Nutritional Values (per serving):

- Calories: 200
- Fat: 14g
- Carbohydrates: 15g
- Protein: 4g

Baked Tilapia with Mango Salsa

Ingredients:

- 2 tilapia fillets
- 1 mango, diced
- 1/4 cup red onion, diced
- 1/4 cup red bell pepper, diced
- 1 jalapeño, minced
- 2 tablespoons cilantro, chopped
- 1 lime, juiced
- 1 tablespoon olive oil
- Salt and pepper to taste

Directions:

1. Preheat the oven to 375°F (190°C).
2. Season tilapia fillets with salt and pepper and place on a baking sheet. Drizzle with olive oil.
3. Bake for 15-20 minutes, or until the fish flakes easily with a fork.
4. In a bowl, combine diced mango, red onion, red bell pepper, jalapeño, cilantro, and lime juice. Mix well.
5. Top the baked tilapia with mango salsa.
6. Serve immediately.

Nutritional Values (per serving):

- Calories: 250
- Fat: 10g
- Carbohydrates: 20g
- Protein: 25g

Spaghetti with Turkey Meat Sauce

Ingredients:

- 8 ounces whole wheat spaghetti
- 1 pound ground turkey
- 2 cups marinara sauce
- 1 onion, chopped
- 2 garlic cloves, minced
- 1 tablespoon olive oil
- 1 teaspoon dried oregano
- 1/2 teaspoon red pepper flakes
- Salt and pepper to taste

Directions:

1. Cook whole wheat spaghetti according to package instructions. Drain and set aside.
2. In a large skillet, heat olive oil over medium heat. Add chopped onion and minced garlic, and sauté until softened.
3. Add ground turkey and cook until browned.
4. Stir in marinara sauce, dried oregano, red pepper flakes, salt, and pepper. Simmer for 10-15 minutes.
5. Toss the cooked spaghetti with the turkey meat sauce.
6. Serve hot.

Nutritional Values (per serving):

- Calories: 400
- Fat: 14g
- Carbohydrates: 45g
- Protein: 25g

Roast Chicken with Carrots and Potatoes

Ingredients:

- 1 whole chicken
- 4 carrots, chopped
- 4 potatoes, chopped
- 2 tablespoons olive oil
- 2 garlic cloves, minced
- 1 tablespoon rosemary, chopped
- Salt and pepper to taste

Directions:

1. Preheat the oven to 375°F (190°C).
2. Place the whole chicken in a roasting pan. Arrange chopped carrots and potatoes around the chicken.
3. In a small bowl, mix olive oil, minced garlic, chopped rosemary, salt, and pepper. Rub the mixture all over the chicken and vegetables.
4. Roast for 1 hour and 30 minutes, or until the internal temperature of the chicken reaches 165°F (75°C).
5. Let the chicken rest for 10 minutes before carving.
6. Serve hot.

Nutritional Values (per serving):

- Calories: 500
- Fat: 25g
- Carbohydrates: 30g
- Protein: 40g

Ratatouille with Baked Polenta

Ingredients:

- 1 eggplant, chopped
- 1 zucchini, chopped
- 1 bell pepper, chopped
- 1 onion, chopped
- 2 garlic cloves, minced
- 2 cups diced tomatoes
- 1 tablespoon olive oil
- 1 teaspoon dried thyme
- 1 teaspoon dried basil
- Salt and pepper to taste
- 1 tube polenta, sliced

Directions:

1. Preheat the oven to 375°F (190°C).
2. In a large pot, heat olive oil over medium heat. Add onion and garlic, and sauté until softened.
3. Stir in eggplant, zucchini, and bell pepper. Cook for 10 minutes.

4. Add diced tomatoes, dried thyme, dried basil, salt, and pepper. Simmer for 20 minutes.
5. Arrange polenta slices on a baking sheet and bake for 15 minutes, or until golden brown.
6. Serve the ratatouille over the baked polenta slices.
7. Serve hot.

Nutritional Values (per serving):

- Calories: 250
- Fat: 10g
- Carbohydrates: 35g
- Protein: 5g

Vegetarian Tacos with Grilled Veggies and Black Beans

Ingredients:

- 1 bell pepper, sliced
- 1 zucchini, sliced
- 1 red onion, sliced
- 1 cup black beans, drained and rinsed
- 1 tablespoon olive oil
- 1 teaspoon cumin
- 1 teaspoon chili powder
- Salt and pepper to taste
- 8 small corn tortillas
- Optional toppings: avocado, salsa, cilantro, lime wedges

Directions:

1. Preheat the grill to medium-high heat.
2. In a bowl, toss sliced bell pepper, zucchini, and red onion with olive oil, cumin, chili powder, salt, and pepper.
3. Grill the vegetables until tender and slightly charred, about 5-7 minutes.
4. Warm the corn tortillas on the grill for about 1 minute on each side.
5. Fill the tortillas with grilled vegetables and black beans.
6. Add optional toppings such as avocado, salsa, cilantro, and lime wedges.
7. Serve immediately.

Nutritional Values (per serving):

- Calories: 200
- Fat: 6g
- Carbohydrates: 30g
- Protein: 6g

Shrimp and Grits with a Light Cajun Sauce

Ingredients:

- 1 pound shrimp, peeled and deveined
- 1 cup grits
- 4 cups water
- 1/2 cup low-fat milk
- 1 tablespoon olive oil

- 2 garlic cloves, minced
- 1 teaspoon Cajun seasoning
- 1 tablespoon lemon juice
- Salt and pepper to taste
- 2 green onions, chopped

Directions:

1. Bring water to a boil in a pot. Stir in grits and reduce heat to low. Cook, stirring occasionally, until thickened, about 20 minutes. Stir in low-fat milk and season with salt and pepper.
2. Heat olive oil in a skillet over medium heat. Add garlic and cook until fragrant, about 1 minute.
3. Add shrimp and Cajun seasoning. Cook until shrimp are pink and opaque, about 3-4 minutes.
4. Stir in lemon juice and remove from heat.
5. Serve shrimp over grits and garnish with chopped green onions.
6. Serve immediately.

Nutritional Values (per serving):

- Calories: 350
- Fat: 10g
- Carbohydrates: 40g
- Protein: 25g

Thai Green Curry with Vegetables

Ingredients:

- 1 tablespoon green curry paste
- 1 can (14 oz) coconut milk
- 1 cup broccoli florets
- 1 cup sliced bell peppers
- 1 cup snap peas
- 1 cup sliced carrots
- 1 tablespoon olive oil
- 1 tablespoon soy sauce
- 1 teaspoon brown sugar
- Fresh basil leaves for garnish
- Cooked jasmine rice for serving

Directions:

1. Heat olive oil in a large pot over medium heat. Add green curry paste and cook for 1 minute.
2. Stir in coconut milk, soy sauce, and brown sugar. Bring to a simmer.
3. Add broccoli, bell peppers, snap peas, and carrots. Simmer until vegetables are tender, about 10 minutes.
4. Serve curry over cooked jasmine rice and garnish with fresh basil leaves.
5. Serve hot.

Nutritional Values (per serving):

- Calories: 300
- Fat: 18g

- Carbohydrates: 30g
- Protein: 6g

Pan-Seared Duck Breast with Orange Sauce

Ingredients:

2 duck breasts

- 1/2 cup orange juice
- 1/4 cup chicken broth
- 2 tablespoons honey
- 1 tablespoon soy sauce
- 1 teaspoon cornstarch
- 1 tablespoon water
- Salt and pepper to taste

Directions:

1. Score the skin of the duck breasts and season with salt and pepper.
2. Heat a skillet over medium-high heat. Place duck breasts skin-side down and cook until the skin is crispy, about 6-8 minutes. Flip and cook for another 4-5 minutes for medium-rare.
3. Remove duck from the skillet and let rest.
4. In the same skillet, add orange juice, chicken broth, honey, and soy sauce. Bring to a simmer.
5. Mix cornstarch and water to make a slurry. Add to the skillet and cook until the sauce thickens.
6. Slice the duck breasts and drizzle with orange sauce.
7. Serve hot.

Nutritional Values (per serving):

- Calories: 400
- Fat: 20g
- Carbohydrates: 15g
- Protein: 35g

Seared Scallops with Quinoa Salad

Ingredients:

- 1 -pound scallops
- 1 cup quinoa
- 2 cups water
- 1/2 cup cherry tomatoes, halved
- 1/4 cup red onion, diced
- 1/4 cup fresh parsley, chopped
- 2 tablespoons olive oil
- 1 lemon, juiced
- Salt and pepper to taste

Directions:

1. Rinse quinoa under cold water. In a pot, bring 2 cups of water to a boil. Add quinoa, reduce heat, and simmer for 15 minutes or until water is absorbed. Fluff with a fork and let cool.
2. In a bowl, combine cooked quinoa, cherry tomatoes, red onion, and parsley.

3. In a skillet, heat olive oil over medium-high heat. Season scallops with salt and pepper. Sear scallops for 2-3 minutes on each side until golden brown.
4. In a small bowl, whisk together lemon juice, olive oil, salt, and pepper. Pour over quinoa salad and toss to combine.
5. Serve seared scallops on top of the quinoa salad.
6. Serve immediately.

Nutritional Values (per serving):

- Calories: 350
- Fat: 12g
- Carbohydrates: 30g
- Protein: 30g

Grilled Vegetables and Farro Salad

Ingredients:

- 1 cup farro
- 2 cups water
- 1 zucchini, sliced
- 1 bell pepper, sliced
- 1 red onion, sliced
- 1 tablespoon olive oil
- 1 tablespoon balsamic vinegar
- 1/4 cup feta cheese, crumbled
- 1/4 cup fresh basil, chopped
- Salt and pepper to taste

Directions:

1. Rinse farro under cold water. In a pot, bring 2 cups of water to a boil. Add farro, reduce heat, and simmer for 20-25 minutes or until tender. Drain and let cool.
2. Preheat the grill to medium-high heat. Toss zucchini, bell pepper, and red onion with olive oil, salt, and pepper. Grill until tender and slightly charred, about 5-7 minutes.
3. In a large bowl, combine cooked farro, grilled vegetables, balsamic vinegar, feta cheese, and fresh basil. Toss to combine.
4. Serve immediately.

Nutritional Values (per serving):

- Calories: 300
- Fat: 12g
- Carbohydrates: 40g
- Protein: 8g

Roasted Turkey Breast with Low-Fat Gravy

Ingredients:

- 1 turkey breast
- 2 tablespoons olive oil
- 1 teaspoon thyme
- 1 teaspoon rosemary
- Salt and pepper to taste

- 2 cups low-sodium chicken broth
- 1 tablespoon cornstarch
- 1/4 cup water

Directions:

1. Preheat the oven to 375°F (190°C).
2. Rub turkey breast with olive oil, thyme, rosemary, salt, and pepper. Place in a roasting pan.
3. Roast for 1 hour and 30 minutes, or until the internal temperature reaches 165°F (75°C).
4. Remove turkey from the oven and let rest.
5. In a saucepan, bring chicken broth to a simmer. Mix cornstarch and water to make a slurry. Whisk into the broth and cook until the gravy thickens.
6. Slice the turkey breast and serve with low-fat gravy.
7. Serve hot.

Nutritional Values (per serving):

- Calories: 250
- Fat: 10g
- Carbohydrates: 5g
- Protein: 35g

Thank You for Continuing This Journey With, Us!

As you delve deeper into the content, we hope you are finding practical tips that aid in your recovery and adjustment. Your perspective is crucial to us and could be a guiding light for others on similar paths. Please consider sharing your experiences by writing a review on Amazon.

Why Your Review Matters:

Your insights not only help us refine our content to better serve you but also empower others exploring similar paths. Every review contributes to a broader community understanding and support.

How You Can Share Your Review:

Through Amazon.com:

Go to the Amazon page where you found my book.

Navigate to the 'Customer Reviews' section.

Click on 'Write a customer review' to share your valuable insights.

Instant QR Code Access: Simply scan the QR code below with your smartphone to be directed to the Amazon review section.

SNACKS

Carrot and Celery Sticks with Hummus

Ingredients:

- 2 large carrots, peeled and cut into sticks
- 2 celery stalks, cut into sticks
- 1 cup hummus

Directions:

1. Arrange carrot and celery sticks on a plate.
2. Place hummus in a small bowl.
3. Serve carrot and celery sticks with hummus for dipping.

Nutritional Values (per serving):

- Calories: 150
- Fat: 8g
- Carbohydrates: 15g
- Protein: 5g

Greek Yogurt with Honey and Almonds

Ingredients:

- 1 cup Greek yogurt
- 1 tablespoon honey
- 2 tablespoons sliced almonds

Directions:

1. Scoop Greek yogurt into a bowl.
2. Drizzle honey over the yogurt.
3. Sprinkle sliced almonds on top.
4. Serve immediately.

Nutritional Values (per serving):

- Calories: 200
- Fat: 8g
- Carbohydrates: 20g
- Protein: 14g

Sliced Apple with Low-Fat Peanut Butter

Ingredients:

- 1 apple, sliced
- 2 tablespoons low-fat peanut butter

Directions:

1. Slice the apple into wedges.
2. Arrange apple slices on a plate.
3. Serve with low-fat peanut butter for dipping.

Nutritional Values (per serving):

- Calories: 180
- Fat: 8g
- Carbohydrates: 25g

- Protein: 4g

Mixed Nuts and Raisins

Ingredients:

- 1/4 cup mixed nuts
- 1/4 cup raisins

Directions:

1. Combine mixed nuts and raisins in a bowl.
2. Serve immediately.

Nutritional Values (per serving):

- Calories: 200
- Fat: 12g
- Carbohydrates: 22g
- Protein: 5g

Fresh Fruit Salad

Ingredients:

- 1 cup strawberries, hulled and sliced
- 1 cup blueberries
- 1 cup pineapple, diced
- 1 cup grapes, halved
- 1 tablespoon lemon juice

Directions:

1. In a large bowl, combine strawberries, blueberries, pineapple, and grapes.
2. Drizzle with lemon juice and toss gently to combine.
3. Serve immediately.

Nutritional Values (per serving):

- Calories: 100
- Fat: 0g
- Carbohydrates: 25g
- Protein: 1g

Guacamole with Whole Wheat Pita Chips

Ingredients:

- 2 ripe avocados
- 1 lime, juiced
- 1/4 cup red onion, diced
- 1/4 cup cilantro, chopped
- Salt and pepper to taste
- 4 whole wheat pitas, cut into chips

Directions:

1. Mash avocados in a bowl.
2. Stir in lime juice, red onion, cilantro, salt, and pepper.
3. Arrange whole wheat pita chips on a plate.
4. Serve guacamole with pita chips for dipping.

Nutritional Values (per serving):

- Calories: 300
- Fat: 18g
- Carbohydrates: 32g
- Protein: 6g

Edamame with Sea Salt

Ingredients:

- 1 cup edamame, in pods
- 1/2 teaspoon sea salt

Directions:

1. Boil edamame in salted water for 5 minutes.
2. Drain and sprinkle with sea salt.
3. Serve immediately.

Nutritional Values (per serving):

- Calories: 150
- Fat: 5g
- Carbohydrates: 12g
- Protein: 12g

Cottage Cheese with Sliced Tomato

Ingredients:

- 1 cup cottage cheese
- 1 tomato, sliced
- Salt and pepper to taste

Directions:

1. Scoop cottage cheese into a bowl.
2. Arrange tomato slices on top.
3. Season with salt and pepper.
4. Serve immediately.

Nutritional Values (per serving):

- Calories: 150
- Fat: 5g
- Carbohydrates: 10g

- Protein: 20g

Baked Kale Chips

Ingredients:

- 1 bunch kale, washed and torn into bite-sized pieces
- 1 tablespoon olive oil
- Salt to taste

Directions:

1. Preheat the oven to 350°F (175°C).
2. Toss kale pieces with olive oil and salt in a large bowl.
3. Spread kale pieces in a single layer on a baking sheet.
4. Bake for 10-15 minutes, or until crispy but not burnt.
5. Serve immediately.

Nutritional Values (per serving):

- Calories: 50
- Fat: 2g
- Carbohydrates: 7g
- Protein: 2g

Cucumber Rounds with Dill Cream Cheese

Ingredients:

- 1 cucumber, sliced into rounds
- 1/4 cup low-fat cream cheese
- 1 tablespoon fresh dill, chopped
- Salt and pepper to taste

Directions:

1. In a bowl, mix low-fat cream cheese with fresh dill, salt, and pepper.
2. Spread a small amount of dill cream cheese on each cucumber round.
3. Arrange on a plate and serve immediately.

Nutritional Values (per serving):

- Calories: 80
- Fat: 5g
- Carbohydrates: 6g
- Protein: 2g

Peanut Butter and Banana Slices

Ingredients:

- 1 banana, sliced
- 2 tablespoons peanut butter

Directions:

1. Slice the banana into rounds.
2. Spread peanut butter on top of each banana slice.
3. Arrange on a plate and serve immediately.

Nutritional Values (per serving):

- Calories: 200
- Fat: 12g
- Carbohydrates: 24g
- Protein: 4g

Zucchini and Parmesan Crisps

Ingredients:

- 2 zucchinis, sliced into rounds
- 1/4 cup grated Parmesan cheese
- 1 tablespoon olive oil
- Salt and pepper to taste

Directions:

1. Preheat the oven to 400°F (200°C).
2. Toss zucchini slices with olive oil, salt, and pepper in a bowl.
3. Arrange zucchini slices on a baking sheet and sprinkle with Parmesan cheese.
4. Bake for 15-20 minutes, or until crispy and golden brown.
5. Serve immediately.

Nutritional Values (per serving):

- Calories: 100
- Fat: 5g
- Carbohydrates: 8g
- Protein: 5g

Popcorn Sprinkled with Nutritional Yeast

Ingredients:

- 1/4 cup popcorn kernels
- 1 tablespoon olive oil
- 2 tablespoons nutritional yeast
- Salt to taste

Directions:

1. Heat olive oil in a large pot over medium heat.
2. Add popcorn kernels and cover with a lid.
3. Shake the pot occasionally until popping slows down.
4. Remove from heat and transfer popcorn to a large bowl.
5. Sprinkle with nutritional yeast and salt, and toss to coat evenly.
6. Serve immediately.

Nutritional Values (per serving):

- Calories: 120
- Fat: 5g
- Carbohydrates: 18g
- Protein: 3g

Roasted Chickpeas with Smoked Paprika

Ingredients:

- 1 can chickpeas, drained and rinsed
- 1 tablespoon olive oil
- 1 teaspoon smoked paprika
- Salt to taste

Directions:

1. Preheat the oven to 400°F (200°C).
2. Toss chickpeas with olive oil, smoked paprika, and salt in a bowl.
3. Spread chickpeas in a single layer on a baking sheet.
4. Roast for 20-30 minutes, or until crispy, shaking the pan halfway through.
5. Serve immediately.

Nutritional Values (per serving):

- Calories: 150
- Fat: 7g
- Carbohydrates: 18g
- Protein: 5g

Chilled Mango Slices

Ingredients:

- 1 ripe mango, peeled and sliced

Directions:

1. Peel and slice the mango.
2. Arrange mango slices on a plate.
3. Chill in the refrigerator for at least 30 minutes before serving.
4. Serve cold.

Nutritional Values (per serving):

- Calories: 100
- Fat: 0g
- Carbohydrates: 25g
- Protein: 1g

DESSERTS

Baked Apple with Cinnamon

Ingredients:

- 4 apples, cored
- 2 tablespoons brown sugar
- 1 teaspoon ground cinnamon
- 1/4 cup raisins
- 1/4 cup chopped nuts (optional)
- 1/2 cup water

Directions:

1. Preheat the oven to 375°F (190°C).
2. Place cored apples in a baking dish.
3. In a small bowl, mix brown sugar, ground cinnamon, raisins, and chopped nuts (if using).
4. Fill the center of each apple with the mixture.

Pour water into the baking dish.

- Bake for 30-35 minutes, or until apples are tender.
- Serve warm.

Nutritional Values (per serving):

- Calories: 150
- Fat: 2g
- Carbohydrates: 35g
- Protein: 1g

Raspberry Sorbet

Ingredients:

- 4 cups raspberries, fresh or frozen
- 1/2 cup sugar
- 1/2 cup water
- 1 tablespoon lemon juice

Directions:

1. In a saucepan, combine sugar and water. Heat until sugar is dissolved to make a simple syrup.
2. Let the simple syrup cool to room temperature.
3. In a blender, combine raspberries, simple syrup, and lemon juice. Blend until smooth.
4. Strain the mixture through a fine sieve to remove seeds.
5. Pour the mixture into an ice cream maker and freeze according to the manufacturer's instructions.

6. Serve immediately or transfer to a container and freeze until firm.

Nutritional Values (per serving):

- Calories: 100
- Fat: 0g
- Carbohydrates: 25g
- Protein: 1g

Pineapple and Kiwi Fruit Tart

Ingredients:

- 1 pre-baked tart shell
- 1 cup pineapple, chopped
- 2 kiwis, peeled and sliced
- 1/2 cup low-fat cream cheese
- 1 tablespoon honey

Directions:

1. Spread low-fat cream cheese evenly over the pre-baked tart shell.
2. Arrange pineapple chunks and kiwi slices on top of the cream cheese.
3. Drizzle honey over the fruit.
4. Chill in the refrigerator for 1 hour before serving.

Nutritional Values (per serving):

- Calories: 200
- Fat: 8g
- Carbohydrates: 30g
- Protein: 4g

Poached Pears with Vanilla

Ingredients:

- 4 pears, peeled and cored
- 4 cups water
- 1/2 cup sugar
- 1 vanilla bean, split and seeds scraped
- 1 tablespoon lemon juice

Directions:

1. In a large pot, combine water, sugar, vanilla bean, and lemon juice. Bring to a simmer.
2. Add pears and simmer for 20-25 minutes, or until pears are tender.
3. Remove pears from the poaching liquid and let cool.
4. Serve the poached pears warm or chilled.

Nutritional Values (per serving):

- Calories: 150
- Fat: 0g
- Carbohydrates: 38g
- Protein: 1g

Angel Food Cake with Fresh Berries

Ingredients:

- 1 store-bought angel food cake
- 2 cups mixed fresh berries (strawberries, blueberries, raspberries)

- 1 tablespoon sugar
- 1/2 teaspoon lemon zest

Directions:

1. Slice the angel food cake into servings.
2. In a bowl, combine fresh berries, sugar, and lemon zest. Toss gently to combine.
3. Serve each slice of angel food cake topped with the berry mixture.

Nutritional Values (per serving):

- Calories: 150
- Fat: 0g
- Carbohydrates: 35g
- Protein: 3g

Chocolate Avocado Mousse

Ingredients:

- 2 ripe avocados
- 1/4 cup cocoa powder
- 1/4 cup honey
- 1/4 cup almond milk
- 1 teaspoon vanilla extract

Directions:

1. In a blender, combine avocados, cocoa powder, honey, almond milk, and vanilla extract. Blend until smooth.
2. Scoop the mousse into serving bowls.

3. Chill in the refrigerator for at least 1 hour before serving.

Nutritional Values (per serving):

- Calories: 250
- Fat: 15g
- Carbohydrates: 30g
- Protein: 3g

Peach and Blueberry Cobbler

Ingredients:

- 2 cups peaches, sliced
- 1 cup blueberries
- 1/4 cup sugar
- 1 tablespoon lemon juice
- 1 cup whole wheat flour
- 1/4 cup brown sugar
- 1 teaspoon baking powder
- 1/4 teaspoon salt
- 1/4 cup cold butter, cut into pieces
- 1/2 cup low-fat milk

Directions:

1. Preheat the oven to 375°F (190°C).
2. In a bowl, combine peaches, blueberries, sugar, and lemon juice. Pour into a baking dish.
3. In another bowl, mix whole wheat flour, brown sugar, baking powder, and salt.

4. Cut in cold butter until the mixture resembles coarse crumbs.
5. Stir in low-fat milk until just combined.
6. Drop the batter by spoon fuls over the fruit mixture.
7. Bake for 30-35 minutes, or until the top is golden brown and the fruit is bubbly.
8. Serve warm.

Nutritional Values (per serving):

- Calories: 250
- Fat: 8g
- Carbohydrates: 42g
- Protein: 4g

Baked Ricotta with Honey and Fig

Ingredients:

- 1 cup ricotta cheese
- 2 tablespoons honey
- 4 figs, sliced
- 1 teaspoon fresh thyme, chopped

Directions:

1. Preheat the oven to 375°F (190°C).
2. Place ricotta cheese in a small baking dish.
3. Drizzle honey over the ricotta.
4. Arrange fig slices on top.
5. Sprinkle with fresh thyme.

6. Bake for 20 minutes, or until the ricotta is slightly golden and the figs are tender.
7. Serve warm.

Nutritional Values (per serving):

- Calories: 200
- Fat: 8g
- Carbohydrates: 24g
- Protein: 8g

Carrot Cake with Cream Cheese Frosting

Ingredients:

- 2 cups grated carrots
- 1 1/2 cups whole wheat flour
- 1 cup brown sugar
- 1/2 cup applesauce
- 1/4 cup vegetable oil
- 2 eggs
- 1 teaspoon vanilla extract
- 1 teaspoon baking soda
- 1 teaspoon cinnamon
- 1/2 teaspoon nutmeg
- 1/2 teaspoon salt

Cream Cheese Frosting:

- 1 cup low-fat cream cheese
- 1/4 cup honey
- 1 teaspoon vanilla extract

Directions:

1. Preheat the oven to 350°F (175°C). Grease a 9-inch round baking pan.

2. In a large bowl, combine grated carrots, whole wheat flour, brown sugar, applesauce, vegetable oil, eggs, vanilla extract, baking soda, cinnamon, nutmeg, and salt. Mix until well combined.
3. Pour the batter into the prepared baking pan.
4. Bake for 35-40 minutes, or until a toothpick inserted into the center comes out clean.
5. Allow the cake to cool completely.
6. For the frosting, beat together low-fat cream cheese, honey, and vanilla extract until smooth.
7. Spread the frosting over the cooled cake.
8. Serve immediately.

Nutritional Values (per serving):

- Calories: 250
- Fat: 10g
- Carbohydrates: 38g
- Protein: 4g

Frozen Yogurt with Mixed Berries

Ingredients:

- 2 cups Greek yogurt
- 1/2 cup honey
- 1 teaspoon vanilla extract
- 1 cup mixed berries (strawberries, blueberries, raspberries)

Directions:

1. In a bowl, combine Greek yogurt, honey, and vanilla extract. Mix well.
2. Pour the mixture into an ice cream maker and freeze according to the manufacturer's instructions.
3. Fold in mixed berries before the yogurt is fully frozen.
4. Serve immediately or transfer to a container and freeze until firm.

Nutritional Values (per serving):

- Calories: 150
- Fat: 0g
- Carbohydrates: 28g
- Protein: 8g

Lemon Pudding

Ingredients:

- 2 cups low-fat milk
- 1/2 cup sugar
- 1/4 cup cornstarch
- 1/4 cup fresh lemon juice
- 1 tablespoon lemon zest
- 1 teaspoon vanilla extract

Directions:

1. In a saucepan, combine low-fat milk, sugar, and cornstarch. Whisk until smooth.
2. Cook over medium heat, stirring constantly, until the mixture thickens and comes to a boil.
3. Remove from heat and stir in lemon juice, lemon zest, and vanilla extract.
4. Pour the pudding into serving dishes and chill in the refrigerator for at least 2 hours before serving.

Nutritional Values (per serving):

- Calories: 120
- Fat: 2g
- Carbohydrates: 24g
- Protein: 3g

Strawberry Banana Smoothie

Ingredients:

- 1 banana
- 1 cup strawberries, hulled
- 1/2 cup Greek yogurt
- 1/2 cup almond milk
- 1 tablespoon honey

Directions:

1. In a blender, combine banana, strawberries, Greek yogurt, almond milk, and honey.
2. Blend until smooth.
3. Pour into glasses and serve immediately.

Nutritional Values (per serving):

- Calories: 200
- Fat: 2g
- Carbohydrates: 40g
- Protein: 6g

Coconut Rice Pudding

Ingredients:

- 1 cup jasmine rice
- 2 cups coconut milk
- 1/4 cup sugar
- 1/4 teaspoon salt
- 1 teaspoon vanilla extract
- 1/4 cup shredded coconut

Directions:

1. Cook jasmine rice according to package instructions.
2. In a saucepan, combine coconut milk, sugar, and salt. Heat until the sugar is dissolved.
3. Stir in the cooked rice and vanilla extract. Simmer for 10-15 minutes, or until the mixture thickens.
4. Stir in shredded coconut.
5. Serve warm or chilled.

Nutritional Values (per serving):

- Calories: 300
- Fat: 15g
- Carbohydrates: 40g

- Protein: 4g

Baked Banana with Dark Chocolate Chips

Ingredients:

- 2 bananas, halved lengthwise
- 1/4 cup dark chocolate chips
- 1 tablespoon chopped nuts (optional)

Directions:

1. Preheat the oven to 350°F (175°C).
2. Arrange banana halves on a baking sheet.
3. Sprinkle dark chocolate chips and chopped nuts (if using) over the bananas.
4. Bake for 10-12 minutes, or until the chocolate is melted and the bananas are tender.
5. Serve warm.

Nutritional Values (per serving):

- Calories: 200

- Fat: 8g
- Carbohydrates: 34g
- Protein: 2g

Watermelon and Mint Salad

Ingredients:

- 4 cups watermelon, cubed
- 2 tablespoons fresh mint, chopped
- 1 tablespoon lime juice

Directions:

- In a large bowl, combine watermelon cubes, fresh mint, and lime juice.
- Toss gently to combine.
- Serve chilled.

Nutritional Values (per serving):

- Calories: 50
- Fat: 0g
- Carbohydrates: 12g
- Protein: 1g

BONUS CHAPTER

ESSENTIAL RESOURCES FOR YOUR JOURNEY

31-Day Meal Plan

Days 1-10

Day	Breakfast	Lunch	Dinner	Snack
1	Greek Yogurt Parfait with Berries	Grilled Chicken Salad with Mixed Greens	Baked Cod with Lemon and Herbs	Sliced Apple with Low-Fat Peanut Butter
2	Avocado Toast on Whole Grain Bread	Quinoa and Black Bean Stuffed Peppers	Turkey Meatballs with Spaghetti Squash	Mixed Nuts and Raisins
3	Spinach and Mushroom Egg White Omelette	Vegetable Lentil Soup	Grilled Salmon with Steamed Asparagus	Carrot and Celery Sticks with Hummus

Day	Breakfast	Lunch	Dinner	Snack
4	Banana Oatmeal Pancakes	Tuna Salad Stuffed Avocado	Chicken and Broccoli Alfredo with Whole Wheat Pasta	Greek Yogurt with Honey and Almonds
5	Smoothie Bowl with Papaya and Chia Seeds	Turkey and Hummus Wrap	Vegan Chili	Baked Kale Chips
6	Baked Sweet Potato and Poached Eggs	Veggie and Goat Cheese Flatbread	Beef Stir Fry with Bell Peppers and Broccoli	Cucumber Rounds with Dill Cream Cheese
7	Turkey Sausage and Bell Pepper Scramble	Grilled Shrimp and Mango Salad	Spaghetti with Turkey Meat Sauce	Edamame with Sea Salt
8	Quinoa Porridge with Almonds and Apple	Grilled Vegetable and Hummus Tartine	Roast Chicken with Carrots and Potatoes	Cottage Cheese with Sliced Tomato
9	Cottage Cheese with Pineapple and Mint	Sweet Potato and Black Bean Burrito	Ratatouille with Baked Polenta	Fresh Fruit Salad
10	Vegan Blueberry Muffins	Chicken Caesar Salad with Low-Fat Dressing	Lemon Herb Roasted Chicken	Guacamole with Whole Wheat Pita Chips

Days 11-20

Day	Breakfast	Lunch	Dinner	Snack
11	Tofu and Asparagus Frittata	Cold Rice Noodle Salad with Peanut Lime Dressing	Grilled Salmon with Steamed Asparagus	Greek Yogurt with Honey and Almonds
12	Overnight Oats with Pumpkin Spice	Mediterranean Chickpea and Cucumber Wrap	Baked Tilapia with Mango Salsa	Baked Kale Chips
13	Whole Wheat Pancakes with Strawberry Compote	Grilled Vegetable and Hummus Tartine	Turkey Meatballs with Spaghetti Squash	Cucumber Rounds with Dill Cream Cheese
14	Turkey Bacon and Avocado Wrap	Quinoa and Black Bean Stuffed Peppers	Lemon Herb Roasted Chicken	Mixed Nuts and Raisins
15	Almond Butter and Banana Sandwich	Grilled Shrimp and Mango Salad	Ratatouille with Baked Polenta	Fresh Fruit Salad
16	Low-Fat Cheese and Tomato Quesadilla	Chicken Caesar Salad with Low-Fat Dressing	Spaghetti with Turkey Meat Sauce	Edamame with Sea Salt
17	Pear and Walnut Baked Oatmeal	Veggie and Goat Cheese Flatbread	Beef Stir Fry with Bell	Cucumber Rounds with

Day	Breakfast	Lunch	Dinner	Snack
			Peppers and Broccoli	Dill Cream Cheese
18	Spinach and Feta Breakfast Burrito	Tuna Salad Stuffed Avocado	Grilled Tofu with a Ginger Soy Glaze	Carrot and Celery Sticks with Hummus
19	Muesli with Skim Milk and Sliced Peach	Turkey and Hummus Wrap	Chicken and Broccoli Alfredo with Whole Wheat Pasta	Greek Yogurt with Honey and Almonds
20	Egg White and Spinach Breakfast Sandwich	Cold Rice Noodle Salad with Peanut Lime Dressing	Vegan Chili	Baked Kale Chips

Days 21-31

Day	Breakfast	Lunch	Dinner	Snack
21	Greek Yogurt Parfait with Berries	Grilled Chicken Salad with Mixed Greens	Baked Cod with Lemon and Herbs	Sliced Apple with Low-Fat Peanut Butter
22	Avocado Toast on Whole Grain Bread	Quinoa and Black Bean	Turkey Meatballs with Spaghetti Squash	Mixed Nuts and Raisins

Day	Breakfast	Lunch	Dinner	Snack
		Stuffed Peppers		
23	Spinach and Mushroom Egg White Omelette	Vegetable Lentil Soup	Grilled Salmon with Steamed Asparagus	Carrot and Celery Sticks with Hummus
24	Banana Oatmeal Pancakes	Tuna Salad Stuffed Avocado	Chicken and Broccoli Alfredo with Whole Wheat Pasta	Greek Yogurt with Honey and Almonds
25	Smoothie Bowl with Papaya and Chia Seeds	Turkey and Hummus Wrap	Vegan Chili	Baked Kale Chips
26	Baked Sweet Potato and Poached Eggs	Veggie and Goat Cheese Flatbread	Beef Stir Fry with Bell Peppers and Broccoli	Cucumber Rounds with Dill Cream Cheese
27	Turkey Sausage and Bell Pepper Scramble	Grilled Shrimp and Mango Salad	Spaghetti with Turkey Meat Sauce	Edamame with Sea Salt
28	Quinoa Porridge with Almonds and Apple	Grilled Vegetable and Hummus Tartine	Roast Chicken with Carrots and Potatoes	Cottage Cheese with Sliced Tomato
29	Cottage Cheese with Pineapple and Mint	Sweet Potato and Black Bean Burrito	Ratatouille with Baked Polenta	Fresh Fruit Salad

Day	Breakfast	Lunch	Dinner	Snack
30	Vegan Blueberry Muffins	Chicken Caesar Salad with Low-Fat Dressing	Lemon Herb Roasted Chicken	Guacamole with Whole Wheat Pita Chips
31	Greek Yogurt Parfait with Berries	Grilled Chicken Salad with Mixed Greens	Baked Cod with Lemon and Herbs	Sliced Apple with Low-Fat Peanut Butter

Foods to Embrace and Foods to Avoid

Navigating your diet after gallbladder removal can feel like walking through a culinary minefield. Without this key organ, which stores bile necessary for the digestion of fats, you might find yourself having to make significant changes to what you eat. Understanding which foods to embrace and which to avoid is crucial not only for your comfort but also for your health.

Foods to embrace should generally be those that are easy on your digestive system. This means foods that are low in fat and are not heavily spiced. Your body can process these foods more easily without the gallbladder. Lean proteins, such as chicken breast, turkey, and fish, are excellent choices. These provide essential amino acids without too much fat. Similarly, whole grains like brown rice, oats, and whole wheat bread are beneficial as they contribute to your daily fiber intake, promoting good digestive health and preventing constipation, which can sometimes be a side effect of gallbladder removal.

Vegetables are your friends, but it's wise to stick to cooked versions, as raw vegetables may be too fibrous and tough on your system initially.

Steamed, roasted, or sautéed vegetables like carrots, beets, and squash are nutritious options that provide vitamins and minerals without causing undue stress to your digestive system. Fruits are also important but opt for those that are less acidic and lower in fat, like bananas, melons, and apples, which are gentler on a sensitive stomach.

Dairy products can still be part of your diet, but moderation is key. Choose low-fat or fat-free options where possible. Yogurt and cottage cheese are excellent as they contain probiotics, which help maintain a healthy balance of gut bacteria, aiding in digestion and nutrient absorption.

Conversely, foods high in fat can cause significant discomfort and should be limited. Fried foods, buttery pastries, and rich creams stimulate the intestine to contract, which can lead to painful spasms and bloating. Processed foods often contain hidden fats and should also be avoided. Foods that are known to produce gas, such as beans, cabbage, and broccoli, might also cause considerable discomfort, although their impact can vary from person to person.

Spicy foods and heavy seasonings can irritate your digestive system, leading to acid reflux and indigestion. While they might not need to be completely eliminated, it is wise to use these sparingly and be mindful of how your body reacts to them. Similarly, while nuts and seeds are healthy, they are high in fats that could be difficult to digest. If you choose to include them in your diet, do so in small quantities and observe how your body handles them.

Caffeinated beverages and alcohol should be consumed with caution. Both can stimulate the digestive tract, causing discomfort and complications such as heartburn and acid reflux. Opt for decaffeinated versions and limit alcohol intake, focusing instead on staying hydrated with plenty of water throughout the day.

Navigating life without a gallbladder means paying closer attention to what and how you eat. Meals should be smaller and more frequent to avoid overloading your system and to keep your digestion running smoothly. As each person's body reacts differently post-surgery, it's beneficial to keep a food diary. Tracking what you eat and how you feel afterward can help you customize a diet plan that works best for you, allowing you to live comfortably and healthily without a gallbladder.

No Gallbladder Grocery List

Creating a grocery list tailored for a diet without a gallbladder focuses on selecting foods that are easier to digest and lower in fat. Here's a thoughtfully organized list to help you shop efficiently and effectively:

Vegetables

Vegetables are a cornerstone of a healthy post-gallbladder removal diet. They should be rich in fiber but not overly gas-producing:

- Carrots
- Spinach
- Zucchini
- Bell peppers
- Butternut squash
- Green beans
- Sweet potatoes (great for their beta-carotene and fiber content)

Fruits

Opt for fruits that are gentle on the digestive system, avoiding those that are excessively high in acids:

- Bananas
- Apples (sweet varieties like Fuji or Gala)
- Melons (watermelon, cantaloupe, honeydew)
- Pears
- Avocado (in moderation due to higher fat content)
- Peaches (without the skin if necessary)

Proteins

Lean proteins are essential for maintaining muscle without overloading the digestive system:

- Chicken breast (skinless and boneless)
- Turkey breast
- Fish (especially light varieties like tilapia and cod)
- Tofu
- Eggs
- Lentils (as a plant-based protein option that's also rich in fiber)

Dairy and Dairy Alternatives

Low-fat and non-fat dairy products can help maintain calcium levels without causing distress:

- Low-fat yogurt
- Skim milk
- Low-fat cottage cheese
- Almond milk (unsweetened)
- Greek yogurt (low-fat)

Grains

Whole grains provide necessary fiber which aids in digestion and helps maintain steady blood sugar levels:

- Brown rice
- Whole wheat bread
- Oats
- Quinoa
- Barley (a great source of fiber)

Healthy Fats

- While it's important to moderate fat intake, healthy fats are still crucial for overall health:
- Olive oil (for cooking or dressings)
- Avocado oil
- Small portions of nuts like almonds or walnuts
- Flaxseeds (milled, for adding to yogurt or smoothies for omega-3 fatty acids)

Miscellaneous

- Herbal teas (such as peppermint or ginger, which can aid digestion)
- Low-fat broths for cooking and sipping
- Spices such as turmeric and ginger, which can reduce inflammation and aid digestion

This list ensures that you have a well-rounded selection of foods that cater to a diet post-gallbladder removal, helping to minimize discomfort while still enjoying a variety of nutritious foods. Adjust quantities and specific items according to personal tolerance and dietary needs.

Post-Surgery Recovery Tips

Navigating the recovery period after gallbladder surgery can be a daunting task, filled with uncertainties about how to best manage your health and return to normalcy. Understanding the importance of proper care following your procedure is crucial, as it can significantly influence your overall recovery speed and comfort level. Here, we'll explore practical and effective strategies to aid in your recuperation, ensuring you are equipped with the knowledge to support your journey toward healing.

The first and perhaps most critical aspect of recovery is managing pain. After gallbladder surgery, it's common to experience discomfort, particularly around the incision sites. Your doctor will likely prescribe pain medication, and it's important to follow the prescribed dosage.

However, supplementing this with other pain management techniques can be beneficial. Gentle movements and walks can reduce stiffness and improve blood circulation, which aids in healing. Be mindful not to engage in strenuous activities too soon, as this can exacerbate pain and lead to complications.

Attention to your diet immediately following surgery is vital. Your gallbladder plays a crucial role in the digestion of fats, and without it, your body will need to adjust. Start with a liquid diet as recommended by your healthcare provider, gradually introducing soft foods as tolerated. It's advisable to avoid fatty, fried, or spicy foods initially, as these can increase gastrointestinal discomfort. Instead, focus on eating small, frequent meals consisting of easy-to-digest foods like soup, yogurt, and applesauce. Over time, you can reintroduce more solid foods, closely monitoring how your body responds.

Hydration is another key element in your post-surgery care. Surgery can dehydrate you, and maintaining adequate fluid intake is essential for detoxifying your body and promoting healing. Aim to drink plenty of water throughout the day. Avoid beverages that can dehydrate you further, such as those containing caffeine and alcohol, especially in the early stages of recovery.

Rest is a cornerstone of any recovery process. Ensure you get plenty of sleep, as it allows your body to heal and rebuild tissues. Create a comfortable sleeping environment, and allow yourself to take naps during the day if you feel tired. Be aware that too much bed rest can lead to complications such as blood clots. Balancing rest with gentle activity, like short walks around your home, is optimal.

Monitoring your incision sites for signs of infection is crucial. Keep the areas clean and dry, and follow any specific instructions given by your surgeon for care. Signs of infection may include excessive redness, swelling, pus, or if the incision is warm to the touch. Fever and increased pain can also indicate an infection, necessitating prompt contact with your healthcare provider.

Lastly, emotional health is an often -overlooked aspect of recovery. It's normal to feel a range of emotions after surgery, from relief to frustration or sadness. These feelings are valid, and recognizing them as part of the recovery process can aid in your emotional well-being. If you find yourself struggling to cope, don't hesitate to seek support from friends, family, or a professional counselor.

By adhering to these guidelines—managing pain, carefully reintroducing foods, staying hydrated, balancing rest with activity, monitoring your surgical sites, and taking care of your emotional health—you set the stage for a smoother and more efficient recovery. Remember, each person's body is different, and thus, listening to yours and giving it time to adjust without rushing the process is essential. Always follow up with your healthcare provider to discuss any concerns or complications you experience during your recovery. With patience and proper care, you can successfully navigate the post-surgery period and move towards reclaiming your health and lifestyle.

BAM Management

Managing bile acid malabsorption (BAM) effectively requires a multifaceted approach tailored to alleviate the symptoms and maintain quality of life. This condition, often surfacing after gallbladder removal, presents challenges due to the body's impaired ability to reabsorb bile acids efficiently. When bile acids enter the colon rather than being absorbed back into the bloodstream, they can cause a range of digestive symptoms, including diarrhea, bloating, and abdominal pain. Here, we explore several strategies designed to manage this condition and mitigate its impacts on daily life.

One of the first lines of defense against BAM is dietary modification. Since bile acids are primarily involved in the digestion of fats, reducing fat intake can significantly alleviate symptoms. Opt for low-fat foods and avoid high-fat meats, dairy products, and fried foods, which can exacerbate diarrhea and discomfort. Instead, focus on lean proteins, fruits, vegetables, and whole grains, which provide necessary nutrients without overstimulating the digestive system.

In addition to reducing fat intake, incorporating soluble fiber into your diet can be beneficial. Soluble fiber found in foods such as oats, apples, carrots, and flaxseeds can bind to bile acids, reducing their reabsorption and easing symptoms. It's important, however, to increase fiber intake gradually, as too much too quickly can increase gas and bloating.

Another crucial aspect of managing BAM is the use of medications. Bile acid sequestrants, such as cholestyramine, colestipol, or colesevelam, are often prescribed to bind bile acids in the intestines, preventing them from causing irritation and reducing diarrhea. These medications can be effective but may also interfere with the absorption of other medications and vitamins, necessitating careful timing of doses. Always consult with a healthcare provider to determine the best medication plan and ensure it is safely integrated with other treatments.

Hydration is a key component in the management of BAM. Diarrhea and frequent bowel movements can lead to dehydration, making it essential to drink adequate fluids throughout the day. Water is best, but electrolyte solutions or drinks can also be helpful to replace lost salts and minerals. Avoiding caffeinated beverages and alcohol, which can worsen dehydration and symptoms of BAM, is also advisable.

Regular medical monitoring is important for anyone managing BAM, as the condition can fluctuate and change over time. Regular check-ups with a healthcare provider can help monitor the effectiveness of management strategies and adjust them as needed. During these check-ups, it's critical to discuss any ongoing symptoms or side effects of treatment, as well as any concerns about nutrient absorption or vitamin deficiencies.

Lastly, lifestyle modifications can also play a significant role in managing BAM. Regular, moderate exercise can help regulate bowel movements and reduce stress, which in itself can exacerbate symptoms. Stress management techniques such as mindfulness, meditation, and yoga can also be beneficial in managing the psychological impacts of living with a chronic digestive condition.

Implementing these strategies requires patience and persistence. Each individual's response to different treatments can vary, making it necessary to adopt a trial-and-error approach to determine what works best for your body. Support from dietitians, physicians, and possibly mental health professionals can provide guidance and improve outcomes. Managing BAM is not only about alleviating physical symptoms but also about improving overall well-being and quality of life, making a comprehensive and informed approach essential.

Supplements Guide

After undergoing surgery, especially one as significant as gallbladder removal, the body's ability to digest and absorb nutrients efficiently can be compromised. To address these challenges and ensure the body receives the necessary nutrients for optimal healing and function, incorporating certain supplements into your daily routine can be beneficial. This guide delves into the recommended supplements and their specific benefits in the post-surgery recovery phase, helping you make informed decisions to support your health.

Firstly, Vitamin D is crucial, particularly because the gallbladder is involved in the digestion of fats, and vitamin D is a fat-soluble vitamin. After gallbladder removal, the body may not absorb fat-soluble vitamins as effectively, which can lead to deficiencies. Vitamin D is essential for bone health, immune function, and anti-inflammatory benefits. Ensuring adequate intake through supplements can help compensate for any decrease in absorption and support overall well-being.

Calcium is another important supplement post-surgery. It works synergistically with vitamin D to enhance bone strength and density. Post-surgery recovery often involves reduced physical activity, which can weaken bones. Supplementing with calcium helps prevent bone loss and maintains skeletal health, particularly if your diet lacks adequate dairy intake or if you're lactose intolerant.

Magnesium plays a pivotal role in numerous biochemical reactions in the body, including muscle and nerve function, regulating blood pressure, and supporting the immune system. It also helps in the absorption of calcium, contributing further to bone health. Many individuals do not get enough magnesium in their diet, so supplementing with it post-surgery can aid in recovery and overall health.

Omega-3 fatty acids, commonly found in fish oil supplements, are essential because they help regulate inflammation—a common issue post-surgery. Omega-3s can help reduce post-operative swelling and pain, support heart health, and improve mood. Since high-fat meals can be challenging to digest post-gallbladder removal, supplementing with fish oil provides a way to obtain essential fats without taxing the digestive system.

Probiotics are beneficial, especially following the administration of antibiotics that are often necessary during and after surgery. Probiotics help restore healthy gut flora, which can be disrupted by antibiotic treatment and surgical stress. A healthy balance of gut bacteria aids in digestion and nutrient absorption and supports the immune system. Incorporating a probiotic supplement can help enhance gastrointestinal function and digestion, which is particularly important in the absence of the gallbladder.

Fiber supplements can also be beneficial, particularly if you experience changes in bowel habits, such as diarrhea, which is a common side effect of post-gallbladder surgery. Soluble fiber helps absorb excess bile acids in the colon, which can reduce irritation and improve bowel movements.

However, it's important to increase fiber intake gradually to avoid gas and bloating and ensure adequate water intake to aid in the fiber's effectiveness.

Vitamin B12 is another critical supplement post-surgery. The changes in bile secretion following gallbladder removal can affect the absorption of vitamin B12, which is vital for red blood cell production, brain function, and DNA synthesis. Supplementing with B12 can help prevent deficiency, maintain energy levels, and support the nervous system.

Iron supplements may be necessary, especially for individuals who experience blood loss during surgery. Iron is crucial for forming hemoglobin, which helps carry oxygen in the blood. Low iron levels can lead to fatigue and anemia, so supplementation might be recommended based on individual needs assessed by a healthcare provider.

Each supplement serves a specific purpose in the recovery process and ongoing health maintenance after gallbladder surgery. However, it's important to consult with a healthcare provider before starting any new supplement regimen, particularly to avoid interactions with other medications and to ensure that you are taking the correct dosages based on your individual health needs. Through careful supplementation, you can support your body's healing process, improve your nutritional status, and enhance your overall recovery post-surgery.

Long-term Dietary Management Strategies

Living without a gallbladder necessitates adjustments in one's diet to manage health effectively over the long term. After gallbladder removal, the body continues to produce bile, but it lacks the reservoir to store and concentrate it, which can complicate the digestion of fats. Consequently, adopting a structured dietary plan is crucial to maintain good health and prevent discomfort. Here are several strategies for long-term dietary management without a gallbladder:

Moderate Fat Intake: Without a gallbladder, managing fat intake becomes essential since the direct flow of bile from the liver may not be sufficient to handle large amounts of fat at once. Incorporate healthy fats gradually and in small amounts into your diet. Opt for sources of monounsaturated and polyunsaturated fats, such as avocados, nuts, seeds, and olive oil, which are easier to digest compared to saturated fats found in high-fat dairy and red meat.

Frequent, Smaller Meals: Eating smaller, more frequent meals can prevent the overwhelming effect on your digestive system, which can be particularly sensitive post-surgery. This eating pattern helps manage the workload on your digestive system, ensuring it is not overloaded with excessive amounts of fats or hard-to-digest foods at any one meal.

Incorporate Soluble Fiber: Soluble fiber can help bind bile acids and aid in their excretion, preventing them from irritating the colon, which can lead to diarrhea—common in patients post-gallbladder surgery. Foods rich in soluble fiber include oats, legumes, nuts, seeds, apples, and blueberries. Introducing these foods can help stabilize digestive processes and support overall gut health.

Limit High-Fiber Foods Initially: While fiber is beneficial, it's important to reintroduce high-fiber foods slowly into your diet after surgery. Initially, high-fiber foods can exacerbate bloating and gas. Gradually increasing fiber allows your body to adapt without causing discomfort.

Stay Hydrated: Good hydration is vital for digestion and helps the body process and transport nutrients effectively. Water aids in the digestion of soluble fiber, turning it into gel-like substances that bind with bile acids and fats to improve stool form and frequency.

Avoid Trigger Foods: Certain foods may increase the likelihood of digestive discomfort or diarrhea. Common triggers include very spicy foods, caffeine, chocolate, and very acidic foods. Keeping a food diary can be helpful to identify personal triggers and understand how different foods affect your body.

Consider Bile Acid Binders: In some cases, doctors may recommend medications such as bile acid binders to help manage symptoms of bile acid malabsorption. These medications can prevent irritation by binding excess bile acids, making them less likely to cause diarrhea and discomfort.

Regular Physical Activity: Regular exercise helps maintain healthy digestion by reducing the time it takes food to move through the large intestine, limiting the amount of water absorbed from the stool into the body. It also accelerates your breathing and heart rate, which helps to stimulate the natural contraction of intestinal muscles, assisting in moving stools out quickly.

Educate Yourself About Fat-Soluble Vitamins: The absorption of fat-soluble vitamins (A, D, E, and K) can be impaired without the gallbladder. Consuming a well-balanced diet with an appropriate amount of fat can aid in the absorption of these vitamins. In some cases, supplementation might be recommended by a healthcare provider.

Regular Medical Check-Ups: Periodic check-ups can help monitor how well your body is adjusting without a gallbladder and ensure that your diet is providing necessary nutrients without causing additional health issues. Your doctor may conduct routine blood work to check for deficiencies and ensure your liver is functioning properly.

Implementing these dietary strategies can significantly improve your quality of life after gallbladder removal. By understanding how your body responds to different foods and how to manage fat intake and digestion, you can lead a healthy life without frequent discomfort or nutritional deficiencies.

CONCLUSION

EMBRACING YOUR HEALTHIER FUTURE WITHOUT A GALLBLADDER

Living without a gallbladder is a significant adjustment, one that affects your diet and overall lifestyle. While it may seem daunting at first, adapting to this new way of life can also be an opportunity to embrace healthier eating habits that can profoundly impact your well-being. This journey, although necessitated by surgery, can lead you to discover a more attentive and beneficial relationship with food, ultimately enhancing your quality of life.

The removal of the gallbladder, a small organ under the liver that aids in fat digestion, necessitates that we pay closer attention to what and how we eat. Without this reservoir to regulate the release of bile, digesting large amounts of fat becomes more challenging. This change, while restrictive, encourages the adoption of a diet lower in fats and higher in fruits, vegetables, and whole grains, aligning closely with what nutritionists deem ideal for long-term health.

Adopting such dietary changes can reduce the risk of heart disease, improve gastrointestinal health, and support weight management. Foods rich in fiber, such as fruits, vegetables, and whole grains, help maintain bowel health and prevent constipation and bloating, common issues post-surgery. These foods also play a role in controlling blood sugar levels, which can prevent diabetes and aid in maintaining a healthy weight.

Moreover, a diet low in saturated fats and high in lean proteins can lead to better cardiovascular health. Lean meats, fish, tofu, and legumes not only provide essential nutrients such as iron and protein but also contain less fat, reducing the strain on your digestive system and lowering your cholesterol levels. This is crucial in preventing heart disease and encouraging a healthy circulatory system.

In addition to physical health benefits, maintaining a balanced diet contributes to mental well-being. A diet that includes a variety of nutrients supports brain function and can improve mood and energy levels. Regular intake of omega-3 fatty acids, which are found in fish and flaxseeds, has been shown to reduce the symptoms of depression and anxiety. Also, maintaining steady blood sugar levels through a balanced diet prevents the peaks and troughs that can affect your mood and energy.

The challenge of digesting certain foods post-gallbladder surgery also opens up an opportunity to become more mindful of eating habits. Mindful eating—paying close attention to the flavors, textures, and sensations of your food—can transform your meals into more satisfying and less automatic experiences, encouraging better portion control and greater appreciation of your food.

It is also helpful to remember that dietary changes post-surgery can vary from person to person. What works for one individual may not work for another, making it important to listen to your body and adjust your diet according to how you feel after eating certain foods. This personalized approach helps in developing a diet plan that not only adheres to medical advice but also suits your individual preferences and lifestyle, making it easier to maintain in the long term.

Beyond diet, integrating regular physical activity into your routine can enhance the benefits of a healthy diet and support efficient digestion. Exercise doesn't just burn calories; it also helps to stimulate intestinal transit, which can alleviate some of the digestive symptoms associated with gallbladder removal, such as bloating and gas.

Encouragingly, making these changes does not have to be a solitary journey. Seeking support from nutritionists, joining support groups, or even just involving friends and family can provide encouragement and increase your commitment to maintaining these changes. Sharing your goals and experiences with others can provide motivation and new ideas, helping you to stick to a healthier lifestyle.

Embracing a healthier future without a gallbladder is about making informed choices that benefit your physical and mental health. It involves understanding the implications of your surgery and adapting in ways that not only prevent discomfort but also enhance your overall well-being. With each small step, you can turn the challenge of living without a gallbladder into an opportunity to live a healthier and more vibrant life.

Encouragement for Continued Health and Wellness

Navigating life post-gallbladder surgery is a journey of adaptation and commitment to long-term health and wellness. The absence of this small yet crucial organ necessitates significant adjustments, particularly in your dietary habits. But beyond these immediate changes, embracing a lifestyle that continuously supports your health can bring about profound benefits. It's not merely about adapting to life without a gallbladder; it's about thriving in it.

Embarking on this path requires encouragement, both from within and from others, to maintain the changes you've implemented. It's understandable to experience setbacks or feel overwhelmed by dietary restrictions and adjustments. However, it's essential to view these challenges as stepping stones towards a healthier life rather than obstacles. Encouragement can take many forms, from self-affirmation to support from healthcare professionals, family, and friends. Celebrating small victories, like a day of eating well or feeling good, can significantly boost your morale and commitment.

Moreover, staying informed about your health is vital. Knowledge is empowering—it can alleviate anxieties about symptoms, help you make informed dietary choices, and provide a sense of control over your health. Regular consultations with healthcare providers, staying updated with the latest health information, and possibly joining support groups where you can learn from others' experiences are all proactive steps towards sustaining your health and wellness.

Additionally, incorporating regular physical activity into your routine is essential for continued health. Exercise isn't just beneficial for weight management; it also promotes better digestion, enhances mood, and boosts energy levels. Activities need not be strenuous—regular walks, yoga, swimming, or other moderate exercises can effectively support your digestive system and overall health.

Mental health is equally crucial in the post-surgery healing process. Stress and anxiety can exacerbate digestive issues, making it important to engage in stress-reducing practices such as meditation, deep-breathing exercises, or hobbies that you enjoy. Mental wellness is integral to physical health, especially when dealing with long-term adjustments to your lifestyle.

Lastly, your diet remains a cornerstone of your well-being. With the gallbladder gone, focusing on a well-balanced diet that includes a variety of nutrients will help manage digestion and maintain health. It's beneficial to keep a food diary to track what foods suit you best and to identify any that may cause discomfort. This ongoing process of tuning and adapting your diet not only helps in managing symptoms but also in understanding your body better.

In encouraging continual health and wellness, remember you're not alone. Many have navigated this path successfully, finding not only a return to good health but an improvement in their overall quality of life. With the right approach, support, and information, you can turn the challenge of living without a gallbladder into a catalyst for enduring health and vitality.

Thank You for Completing This Book!

We truly appreciate you taking the time to read through and hope the information has been helpful in your post-gallbladder surgery life. We would be grateful if you could share your thoughts and experiences by leaving a review on Amazon.

Why Your Review Matters:

Your feedback is incredibly important to us. It helps improve the quality of our resources and assists others in making informed decisions about their health and dietary needs.

How You Can Share Your Review:

Through Amazon.com:

- Go to the Amazon page where you found my book.
- Navigate to the 'Customer Reviews' section.
- Click on 'Write a customer review' to share your valuable insights.

Instant QR Code Access: Simply scan the QR code below with your smartphone to be directed to the Amazon review section.